MW01201924

Thera

NEW ASPECTS OF ANTIQUITY

General Editor: COLIN RENFREW

Consulting Editor for the Americas: JEREMY A. SABLOFF

CHRISTOS G. DOUMAS

Thera

Pompeii of the ancient Aegean

Excavations at Akrotiri 1967–79

with 123 illustrations, 15 in color

THAMES AND HUDSON

For Alex

First published in the USA in 1983 by Thames and Hudson Inc., 500 Fifth Avenue, New York, New York 10110

Library of Congress Catalog Card Number 81-86685

Printed and bound in Hungary

Contents

General Editor's foreword 7

Introduction 11

1 The Aegean background 15

GEOLOGICAL HISTORY 15 THE AEGEAN CLIMATE 16 THERA AND AEGEAN MYTHOLOGY 18

2 The Aegean and the Cyclades before the Minoan expansion 22

THE NEOLITHIC BACKGROUND 22 EARLY BRONZE AGE ISLAND CULTURES IN THE AEGEAN 22 THE CYCLADES DURING THE EARLY AND MIDDLE BRONZE AGE 24 THE EARLY AND MIDDLE BRONZE AGE ON THERA 27

3 The site of Akrotiri 29

HISTORY OF THE EXCAVATION 29 AKROTIRI BEFORE LATE CYCLADIC I 42

4 The Late Cycladic city of Akrotiri 45

EXTENT 45 TOWN PLAN AND ARCHITECTURE 50 ART 56 DESCRIPTION OF INDIVIDUAL WALL-PAINTINGS 77 POTTERY 108 STONE INDUSTRY 114 METALLURGY 114 FURNITURE 116 WEAVING 117 SUBSISTENCE 118 TRADE AND COMMUNICATION 118 WRITING AND COUNTING 120 SOCIETY 122

5 Thera and the Aegean in the Late Bronze Age 126

THE MINOAN EXPANSION IN THE AEGEAN 126 THE CYCLADES IN THE LATE BRONZE AGE I PERIOD 127 LATE CYCLADIC I THERA 128 THERA, THE CYCLADES AND THE MINOAN THALASSOCRACY 129 MYCENAEANS ON THERA? 131

6 The end of Late Cycladic I Thera 134

THE ARCHAEOLOGICAL EVIDENCE 134 THE GEOLOGICAL EVIDENCE 136 CHRONOLOGY 138

7 **The Aegean and the eruption of Thera** 140
THERA AND THE DESOLATION OF MINOAN CRETE 140 THERA, THE AEGEAN AND THE EASTERN MEDITERRANEAN 147

8 **Thera and the legend of Atlantis** 151
PLATO'S STORY 151 AGREEMENTS AND DISAGREEMENTS 153

Epilogue: Thera and the Aegean after the eruption 157

Chronological table 159

Select bibliography 160

List of illustrations 162

Index 165

General Editor's foreword

On a summer's day, some thirty-five centuries ago, the central mountain of the beautiful Aegean island of Kalliste burst open with dramatic suddenness to shower its villages and the thriving town on its southern shore with volcanic ash and pumice. With increasing ferocity, in the space probably of just a few days or weeks, the volcano poured out a colossal quantity of material–the ash cloud extended for hundreds of miles–and parts of Kalliste were buried to a depth of 60 m. The whole centre of the island subsided into a vast abyss into which the sea then poured, forming a great volcanic caldera so large that several fleets might anchor there, were not its sides so steep and its base so deep that no anchor can find purchase.

That island we now call Thera, and the caldera forms its well-sheltered harbour (although with moorings since ships still cannot anchor). Its once-thriving town, near the modern village of Akrotiri, has lain buried from the Late Bronze Age of around 1500 BC until the present century. Its rediscovery by the late Professor Spyridon Marinatos and its subsequent investigation by him and by Professor Christos Doumas constitutes one of the great archaeological finds of our era, rivalling in its importance those at Roman Pompeii, buried under the ash of Vesuvius, which so galvanized the scholarly world of eighteenth-century Europe.

Marinatos, already thirty years before his discovery of the Bronze Age town of Akrotiri, wrote a now-famous article suggesting that the end of the civilization of Minoan Crete was brought about by the cataclysmic eruption of the volcano of Thera, in or around the fifteenth century BC. His interest in this question led him to follow up earlier indications on Thera, as Professor Doumas here relates, and to discover what must rank as the most completely preserved prehistoric site in Europe, perhaps in the world. I remember his enthusiasm on that day in 1967, during his first season's work, when my wife and I visited the excavation and saw the rows of painted pottery jars emerging from the fine white ash, still standing upright in just the position that they had been left at the onset of the great catastrophe some thirty-five centuries ago. On a later visit I was privileged to be present as the breathtakingly lifelike wall-painting of swallows in flight, 'The Coming of Spring', was being uncovered–still amazingly in position and preserved entire on the wall in the Room of the Lilies, after so many thousand years. We all realized, I think, that here was one of the most perfect works of art to have been preserved for us from prehistoric times.

Since Marinatos' untimely death in 1974, Professor Christos Doumas, who had already contributed much to the success of the work, has continued the excavation which, as the leading authority on the prehistory of the Cycladic islands, he is uniquely qualified to do. He has consolidated the pioneering successes of those early years, laying the secure and methodical basis for the full recording of what, as his account here makes clear, is an excavation of great complexity with a bewildering abundance of finds.

Time stood still, on that summer day, when the first pungent lapilli of pumice fell. If any last inhabitant remained–for most had fled following the earlier premonitory earthquakes–he must have known that the end had come. Nothing has been disturbed or displaced since the ash-fall. The archaeologist therefore has a unique opportunity: here is no scrap heap of discarded rubbish, as at so many sites, no eroded ruin whose reconstruction requires much argumentation about 'formation processes'. The tools, the pots, and indeed the walls of many of the houses, stand just as they were left by their departing owners: the basement and ground floors are preserved, and sometimes much of the floor above as well. The excavation is therefore a great enterprise of conservation, with the unique opportunity to reveal whole streets of a prehistoric town.

The great joy of Akrotiri is, of course, the mural painting: the principal works so far discovered are here described by Professor Doumas. In contrast to the fragmentary compositions which have come down to us from Minoan Crete–which often owe as much to the taste of the brothers Gilliéron, their restorers, as to the original artists–these are in some cases complete. In other cases, as the author describes, through the special skills of the team of conservators which he has built up, they can be restored so that the spatial relationships of the entire composition can be securely re-established.

Ultimately of at least equal significance to the archaeologist may be the opportunity which the site offers of establishing the original context of use of each and every object on the site, however mundane, so that the full working of a complete prehistoric settlement may be studied and published in satisfying detail. This is an exacting task, and readers of this account of his meticulous work will come to appreciate how fortunate we are that Professor Doumas has had the foresight and the tenacity to develop systems of excavation and recording to cope with the great flow of information from the continuing work of exploration.

In his account here he brings together the full range of evidence for the life of Akrotiri in its heyday, as well as in earlier periods. He reserves for a later chapter the intriguing and controversial question of the possibly catastrophic effects of the great eruption upon the civilization of Minoan Crete. Was Crete devastated by the cataclysm, or was its demise due to other causes? This remains a lively issue: at the First International Conference on Thera in 1969 I found myself one of the small minority of sceptics in this matter. The sceptics are now much more numerous, and I believe that they will find Professor Doumas' careful treatment of the evidence a very just one, as indeed is his dispassionate account of the Atlantis question.

What the future of the excavations may hold we cannot tell. Somewhere on the site there may be the remains of the palace or mansion of its ruler–for I cannot myself quite believe that the Therans so far anticipated their successors of a millennium later as to found a democratic government without centralized, probably hereditary rule. And if that ruler, like his contemporaries in Crete and apparently at Phylakopi on the island of Melos, relied on scribes to administer a well-organized bureaucracy, his archive of clay tablets, written in the Minoan Linear A script, may yet be recovered, perfectly preserved and lightly baked by the enveloping layer of volcanic ash.

No doubt Akrotiri still holds many surprises for Professor Doumas and for us all. But already for the reader, or for anyone who has seen the verve and vitality of the murals, many now displayed in the National Archaeological Museum of Athens, who has walked down the Telchines Road at Akrotiri with its two-storey Bronze Age buildings on each side, or indeed has sailed in the early morning light into that great caldera, its many-layered cliffs sheared vertically by the great collapse, the life and death of this buried town have an immediate reality.

Colin Renfrew

Acknowledgments

I should like to take this opportunity to express my gratitude to the Archaeological Society at Athens for entrusting the continuation of the excavation to me after the sudden death of Professor Spyridon Marinatos in 1974. In particular my thanks go to the Committee of the Society and its Secretary-General, Professor George Mylonas, for their encouragement and support in the multiple problems of the excavation as well as for the use of illustrative material in this book. To the architect of the excavation, Mrs Kallirhoe Palyvou-Mavroeidi, I express especial thanks for her enthusiasm and work. My fellow archaeologists Ch. Sigalas, M. Marthari, Ch. Televandou, and the artists, C. Eliakis and Y. Linardos, have been immensely helpful and cooperative. I am likewise indebted to the restorers of the finds, in particular Tassos Margaritoff, Inspector of Conservation; Stamatis Perrakis, Panayiotis Dritsas, Andreas Stratsianis, Stavros Angelides, Iakovos Michaelides, chief restorers of frescoes; Katerina Eliogamvrou and Vasilis Alefrangis, pottery restorers. Similar thanks should go to all the students and workers who have participated in the excavations at Akrotiri.

Last but not least I want to express my gratitude to my wife, Alex, whose support and encouragement made the writing of this book possible. She also undertook the heavy task of correcting and improving my English text.

Christos G. Doumas

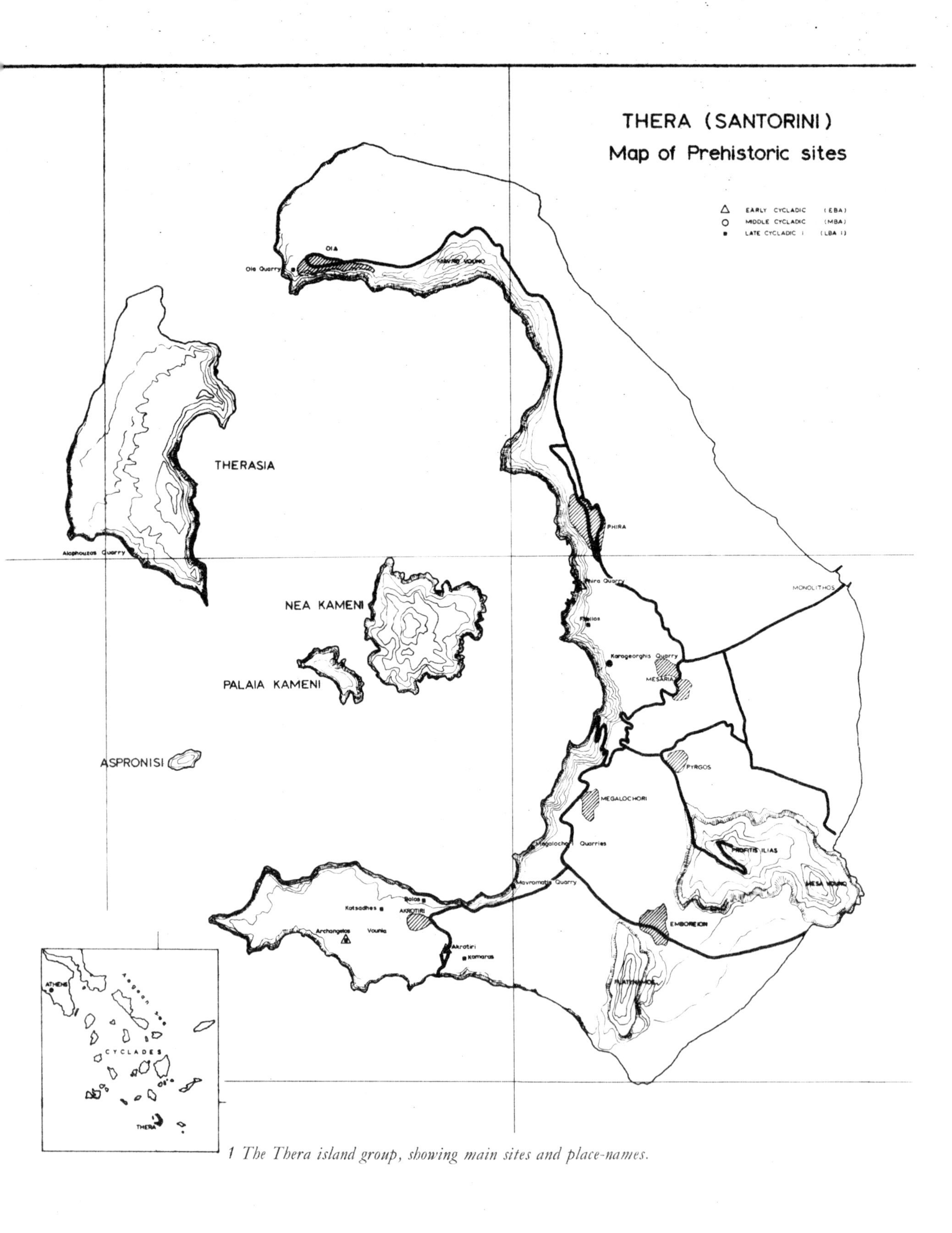

1 The Thera island group, showing main sites and place-names.

Introduction

At the southern tip of the volcanic island of Thera (Santorini), in the Aegean Sea, lies the modern village of Akrotiri. Its name derives from the Greek word for 'cape' or 'promontory', which accurately describes its situation, as it does that of several other similarly named villages in the coastal regions and islands of Greece. The Venetians recognized the strategic importance of the site and erected a citadel on its highest point during their occupation of Thera in the early modern period. From the citadel one has absolute control over the south-western end of the island as well as the plain to the southeast. This strategic position does not seem to have been of great importance in ancient times, however, for the prehistoric site of Akrotiri lies in a lower and flatter area to the south of the present village, not far from the sea. It would appear that proximity to the sea, rather than natural fortifications, determined the location of the original settlement.

figs 1, 2

plate 3

Of all the prehistoric sites identified to date on Thera, that of Akrotiri is the most advantageously situated for maritime activities and agriculture. It dominates the flat southern part of the island and, at the same time, offers an ideal anchorage, sheltered from the almost constantly blowing northerly winds. Even today the bay of Akrotiri is the safest haven for ships in a storm. On clear days in early spring and autumn the island of Crete is visible sixty-nine miles due south, resting 'like a monster upon the sea', as one Greek song puts it. Akrotiri would have been the perfect base for trade with the Cretans from earliest times.

plate I

It was these features of the site which eventually led the Greek archaeologist, Spyridon Marinatos, to excavate in the area. He had conceived the idea that the ancient Minoan civilization on Crete, whose sudden demise in the mid-second millennium BC was unexplained, had been destroyed by the volcanic explosion of Thera in about 1500 BC. Marinatos had first published his theory in the archaeological journal *Antiquity* in 1939, but, as *Antiquity*'s editors noted at the time, the thesis required 'additional support from excavation'. It was 'additional support' that Marinatos came to seek on Thera.

His plans to explore the island were delayed due to the outbreak of the Second World War and later the Greek Civil War. When eventually he returned to the island in the 1960s his first priority was the identification of sites located or partially investigated by previous scholars. This was a difficult task because earlier investigators had left few records of their work and all trace of the excavations of the nineteenth century had been obliterated by ploughing. The only site which proved easy to identify was that of Kamaras in the Valley of Potamos, east of the present dig, thanks to the photographic documentation kept in the archives of the German Archaeological Institute in Athens. Although no archaeological remains were visible, it was possible to locate the site from the configuration of the ground in relation to the village.

plate 4

fig. 2

Much information about the site of Akrotiri can be gleaned from the carefully drawn map published in 1874 by the French scholar, Mamet, in his dissertation 'De insula Thera'. On this map it can be seen that Mamet had in fact excavated at the site of Favatas, on the eastern side of the ravine where the current excavations are taking place. Other evidence as well persuaded Marinatos to start digging here. The late Elias Pelekis from Mesa Gonia had been the guard at the site of ancient Thera (Mesa Vouno)–a mainly Hellenistic city on the southeast corner of the island–at the time when Baron Hiller von Gaertringen was excavating there in the late 1890s. Pelekis recalled that one of von Gaertringen's assistants, R. Zahn, had conducted excavations at Potamos which had also yielded antiquities. He told this to his son, who remembered the story and sometime in the early 1960s paid a visit to Favatas, from where he collected a bagful of sherds. He handed these over to the then Ephor of the Cyclades, Nikolaos Zapheiropoulos, and they were deposited in the Thera Archaeological Museum where Marinatos examined them. Thus the archaeological interest of Favatas was further confirmed.

Another two old men on the island supplied Marinatos with clues. Georgios Saliveros, or Batzanis, from Megalochori, was at the time one of the oldest masons alive on Thera, creator of many beautiful churches in his village and elsewhere. He too had childhood memories of the 'Baron' digging at Potamos and the existence of remains in the area of Favatas. The second person was Stathis Arvanitis, retired field-guard of Akrotiri, who led Marinatos to a spot in the Favatas area where the ground had collapsed. He also told the Professor that in some places ploughing was obstructed by some peculiar masses of stone (these later proved to be the lintel stones of the window above the entrance to the West House). Marinatos was quick to realize that soil subsidence must be due to the collapse of roofs and upper storeys of houses.

Equipped with all this incidental information, Marinatos proceeded to survey the area of Favatas and confirmed what Pelekis, Batzanis and Arvanitis had told him. Moreover, he noticed that the circular troughs which the locals used to water their animals were actually very heavy prehistoric mortars made of local volcanic stone. In view of their size and weight the site from which they had been brought must have been in close proximity.

So, after evaluation of this disparate evidence, Marinatos began digging at Akrotiri in 1967. The results were spectacular, as a glance at the illustrations in this book will confirm. Marinatos' choice of site was fully vindicated, and a programme of excavations was initiated which continues to this day.

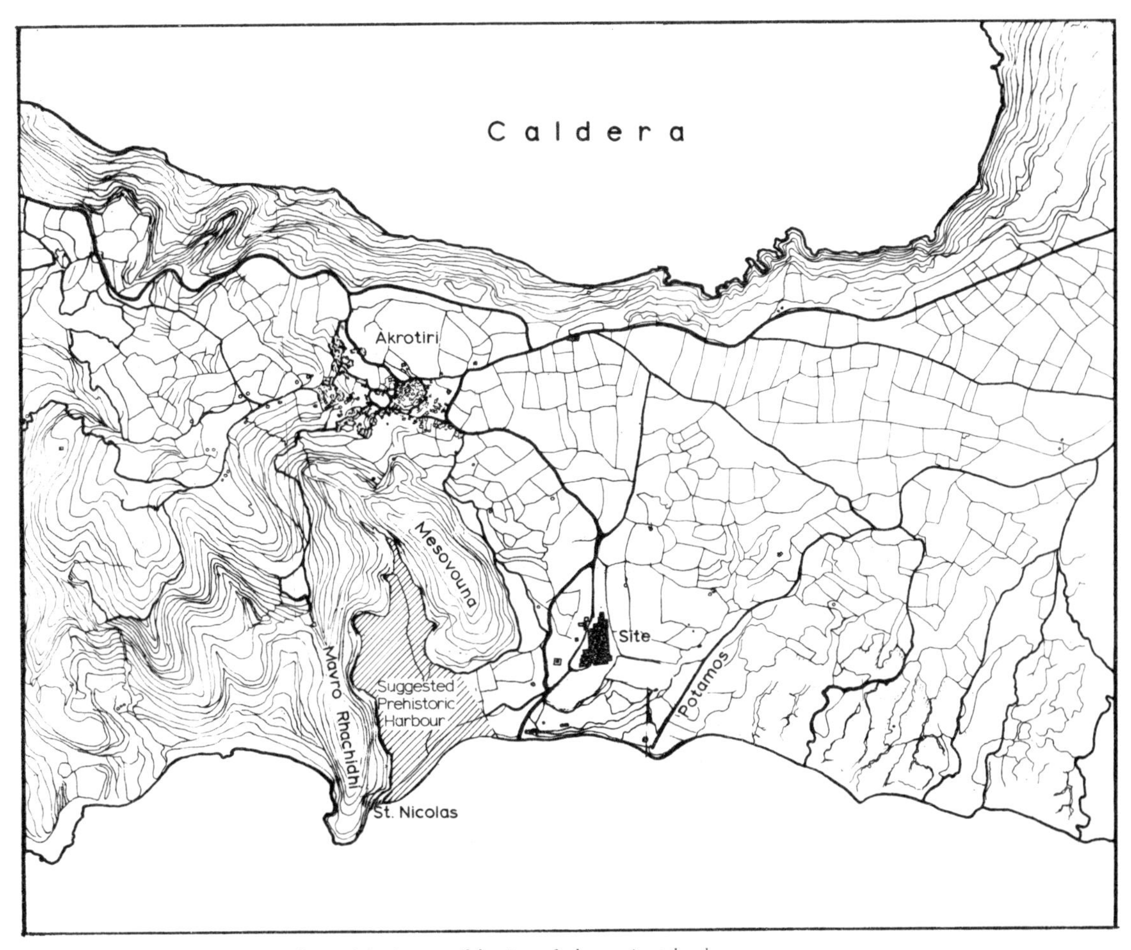

2 The Akrotiri region, together with the possible site of the ancient harbour.

The Greek Archaeological Society sponsored the excavation from the start, with generous financial support from the Greek government. At first Marinatos was assisted by a small group of his students, an architect, the vase-mender and restorer the late Zacharias Kanakis and local workers. In autumn 1968 the author joined the excavation team, taking over the directorship after Marinatos' death in 1974. An architect is now employed on a full-time basis and about a dozen archaeologists assist each season (late June to late September). In addition, specialists such as palaeo-ethnobotanists, metallurgists, zoologists, chemists, biologists and geographers, to name but a few, have joined the vulcanologists and geologists already working on the problems posed by the site.

After Marinatos' death there was a brief pause in the excavations, but actual digging was resumed in 1976. It will take several decades, if not centuries, to excavate the site fully. The aims of the present excavators are not merely to produce impressive finds; these will come anyway. Our ambition now is to complete the exploration of all the buildings uncovered so far–in fact no building has been fully excavated as yet–and thus proceed to the conservation and restoration of the finds. In the meantime this general account of the excavations is provided as a kind of interim report, in the hope that it will bring to a wider public knowledge of the achievements and way of life of an Aegean society three-and-a-half thousand years ago.

Before we delve deeper into the story of the excavation, we must stand back for a moment and examine the history of Thera in its Aegean context. To understand Akrotiri we must first understand the geological, mythological and archaeological background of the Greek islands.

1 The Aegean background

Geological history

The Aegean Sea was formed during the Pliocene Age, about five million years ago, as a result of the fragmentation and collapse of part of the earth's crust. The southern Aegean lies at the junction of two of the tectonic plates–the African and Eurasian–which make up the earth's crust, and friction between these plates threw up a chain of volcanoes. Stretching from Greece to Turkey, the volcanoes form an arc of islands: Aegina, Methana, Poros, Melos, Kimolos, Polyaigos, Pholegandros, Thera, Nisyros and Kos. Each one provided materials which were to play a significant part in the development of Aegean civilization, but historically the most important and interesting among them is Thera.

Thera today is in fact a group of islands (Therasia, Aspronisi, Palaea Kameni, Nea Kameni and Thera proper) which together form part of what was once one giant volcano. The massif of Profitis Elias, in the southeast of the main island (Thera proper), comprises the core of the original island. Around it, beginning some one million years ago according to fission–track dating, several volcanoes became active at various times, the material they disgorged eventually creating a small island, smaller in area than the present insular complex of Thera and Therasia. Because of its circular shape this island has been called *Stronghyle* ('the Round One').

fig. 1

The eruption which occurred in about the middle of the second millennium BC (which Marinatos believed helped destroy Minoan civilization) caused the fragmentation of Stronghyle and the creation, in their present form, of the islands of Thera, Therasia and Aspronisi around the great bay or *caldera*. A long period of calm seems to have lasted for about thirteen centuries. Then, in the middle of the caldera, as Strabo the Geographer reported, 'between Thera and Therasia fires broke forth from the sea and continued for four days, so that the whole sea boiled and blazed, and the fires cast up an island which was gradually elevated as though by levers and consisted of burning masses–an island with a stretch of twelve stadia in circumference' (I. 3. 16). This eruption is dated to 197 BC and the island thus created, called by the contemporary Greeks Hiera ('the Sacred One'), is identified with the islet known today as Palaea Kameni ('the Old Burnt'). Later eruptions resulted in the appearance of more rocky islets in the sea, such as Theia ('Divine'), which appeared in AD 19. A new island also emerged from the depths of the sea in the outburst of AD 726; it seems that the historical city of ancient Thera on Mesa Vouno was showered with pumice. The Byzantine chronicler, Theophanes, wrote an account of this eruption which occurred during the reign of Emperor Leo III the Isaurian. Around AD 1570 Mikra Kameni ('Small Burnt') was formed. Another, well-recorded, eruption took place in AD 1650 under the sea northeast of Koloumbos. Descriptions of its effects around the Aegean are given in contemporary sources (two Cretan poems, the notes of a monk from Patmos, Santorini folk songs and correspondence between Roman Catholic priests on Naxos and Santorini). According to these sources the flames of the eruption were visible in Herakleion, Crete, and pumice floated as far as Leros in the eastern Aegean. Herakleion was under siege by Turkish forces at the time and tidal waves created by the eruption swept away the Turkish ships beached on the island of Dia.

A later period of volcanic activity (1707–11) resulted in the formation of Nea Kameni ('New Burnt') between Palaea and Mikra Kameni. Islets appeared, disappeared and reappeared during the eruptions of 1866–70, 1925–26, 1928, 1939–41 and 1950, all the rocks thus created being united today into Nea Kameni island. The highest peak of the present volcano, King George I, is 130.8 m above sea level. Fumes and gasses issue forth from several vents, quite often at a temperature of 86° C.

The geological stratigraphy of Thera is one of the best studied in the world, thanks to its exposure in the caldera walls. Under the Late Bronze Age layer of pumice and ash (Upper Pumice Series), up to 60 m thick, there are twenty-one alternating pyroclastic strata totalling 35 m in thickness. These strata, resting on a 4-m–deep layer of pumice (Middle Pumice Series), consist of dark ashes, cinders, scoriae, pumice, bombs, xenolithic lapilli, blocks and lahar deposits. Under the Middle Pumice Series layer there is a succession of lava deposits including, near the top, the thick stratum of the Lower Pumice Series. The three large deposits of the Upper, Middle and Lower Pumice Series represent explosions of the island of more or less the same kind. The formation of the Middle Pumice Series is estimated by specialists to have taken place before 37,000 years ago. This date constitutes the terminus after which various palaeosols (ancient soils) were formed on top of the Middle Pumice Series.

The Aegean climate

The Aegean exhibits a considerable variation in climate: the north for instance, is colder than the south and the west is drier than the east. The coastal areas enjoy a milder climate favouring the cultivation of palm trees, olive trees and vines. The Cyclades, from the point of view of climate, constitute a special group among the Aegean islands. They enjoy a dry, mild climate with an average annual humidity of 65 per cent in the southwest islands. Frost is an extremely rare phenomenon, the number of days with frost not exceeding 4–5 per annum. The Cyclades, together with Rhodes and Lesbos, have the longest periods of sunshine in the entire Aegean region (almost 3250 hours each year).

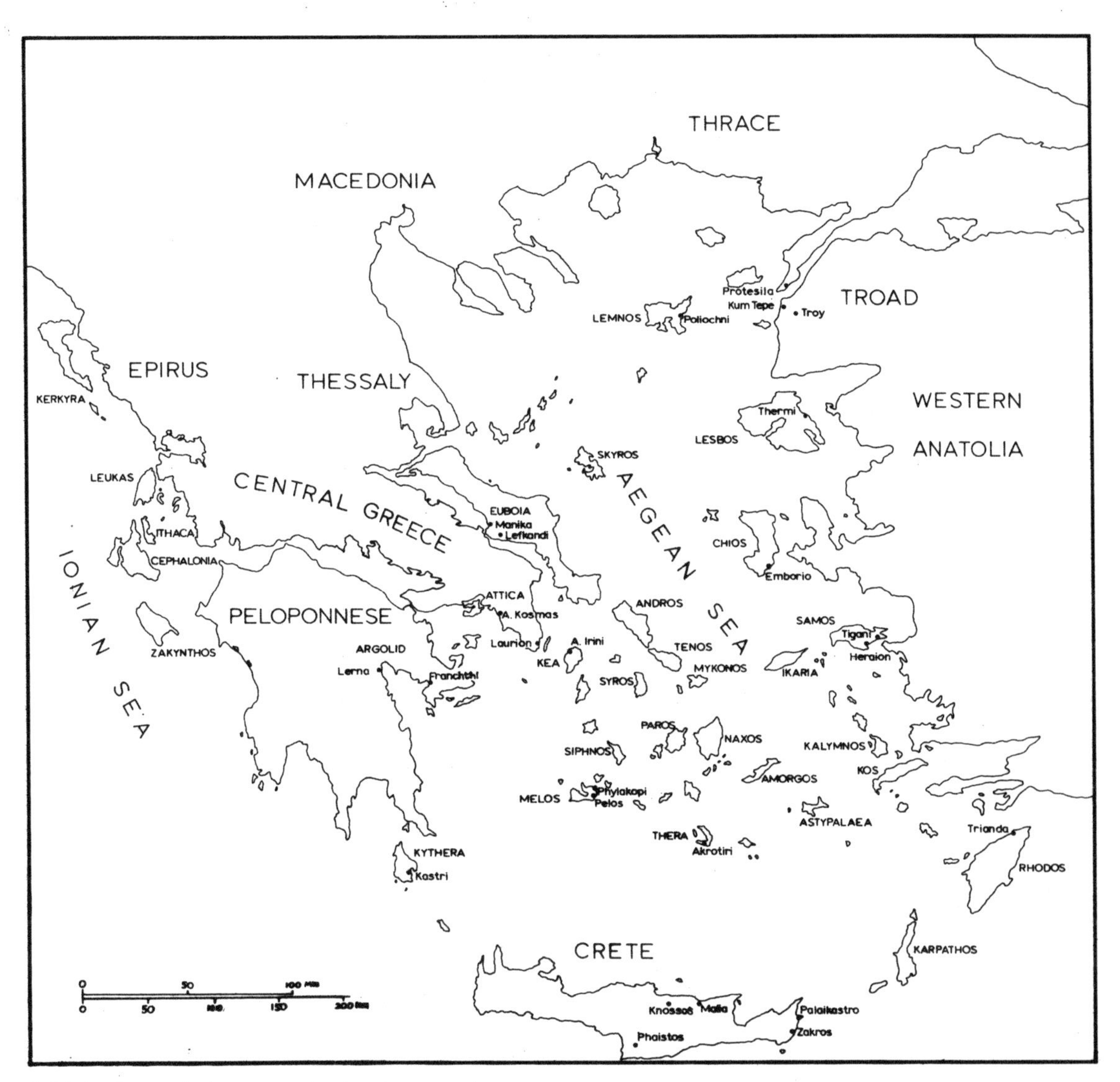

3 Main sites and place-names in the Aegean region.

In general the Aegean is the windiest part of Greece. Throughout the year northerly winds prevail, but in autumn, winter and spring these often alternate with winds from other directions. As a result atmospheric conditions over the Aegean are extremely variable. In summer the regular weather is characterized by the Etesian winds or *meltemi*. These, known even from antiquity, blow from the northeast during the whole period from mid-May to mid-October, and are often so violent that they prevent seafaring and the growth of vegetation. The coastal winds are more severe than those in the open sea. All year, and particularly in winter, precipitous coastal areas suffer from the 'white storms' which are caused very quickly by vertically blowing winds and often reach speeds of

41–45 knots. These storms are of local character and a few miles offshore the sea can be quite calm.

The Cyclades form a rain shadow, thanks to chains of mountains on Crete and the Peloponnese which obstruct the passage of the rain-bearing southerly and westerly winds. Kea, Kythnos, Seriphos, Thera, Ios, Sikinos, Pholegandros, Anaphi and Amorgos are among the driest parts of Greece with a rainfall less than 400 mm a year. The rainfall in the rest of the Cyclades varies between 400 and 600 mm, whilst in the heights of Andros it exceeds 600 mm. The long dry period in the Cyclades lasts from April till almost the end of September.

There seems to have been little change in the climate of the Aegean since prehistoric times, as the fossil plants discovered in the deep volcanic deposits on Thera testify. *fig. 4* Some of the twenty-one alternating pyroclastic strata which lie between the Upper and Middle Pumice Series are decomposed to palaeosols, often containing moulds of roots and thin stems of trees or bushes. In these strata, below the Late Bronze Age palaeosol, eleven plant horizons have been identified. Four of them are rich in fossil plants and contain abundant leaves and rarer fruits of the species *Chamaerops humilis L., Pistacia lentiscus L., Phoenix dactylifera I., Olea europae,* and *Tamarix*. The evidence from moulds is that palms *(chamaerops)* grew on the island and reached a height of about 2–3 m with a stem thickness of 30–40 cm. The dates of three plant bearing palaeosols below the Late Bronze Age palaeosol are *c.* 13,000, 18,000 and 37,000 years ago. This suggests, as the specialist who conducted the research on the Theran plant horizons, Dr W. Friedrich, has pointed out, that in the last 37,000 years the climate in the Mediterranean 'was similar or nearly the same as at present'. All the fossil plant species from the four plant horizons still exist in the Mediterranean and on Thera itself.

Thera and Aegean mythology

The Aegean has been the cradle of various prehistoric civilizations and has provided the setting for several myths and legends recorded by the Greeks in later times. These myths are echoes from a remote past and must to some extent reflect contacts between the various prehistoric peoples in the Aegean and beyond. Many legends emphasize the importance of the Dardanelles straits–the Greek Hellespont–as the gateway to the Black Sea, with which contacts had always been close and intense. The winged golden ram, bearing on its back Phrixus and his ill-fated sister Helle, flew from Mount Laphystium in Boeotia to the land of Colchis on the east coast of the Black Sea. A generation later Jason launched his famous expedition with the Argonauts to bring back from Colchis the golden fleece of Phrixus' ram. Contacts and antagonisms between the south and north *fig. 3* Aegean are reflected in the myths referring to Troy. According to one of them, Troy was founded by Cretans led by Prince Scamander. Conflicts are apparent in the legend of the kidnapping of Helen, wife of Menelaus, King of Sparta, which resulted in the Trojan War.

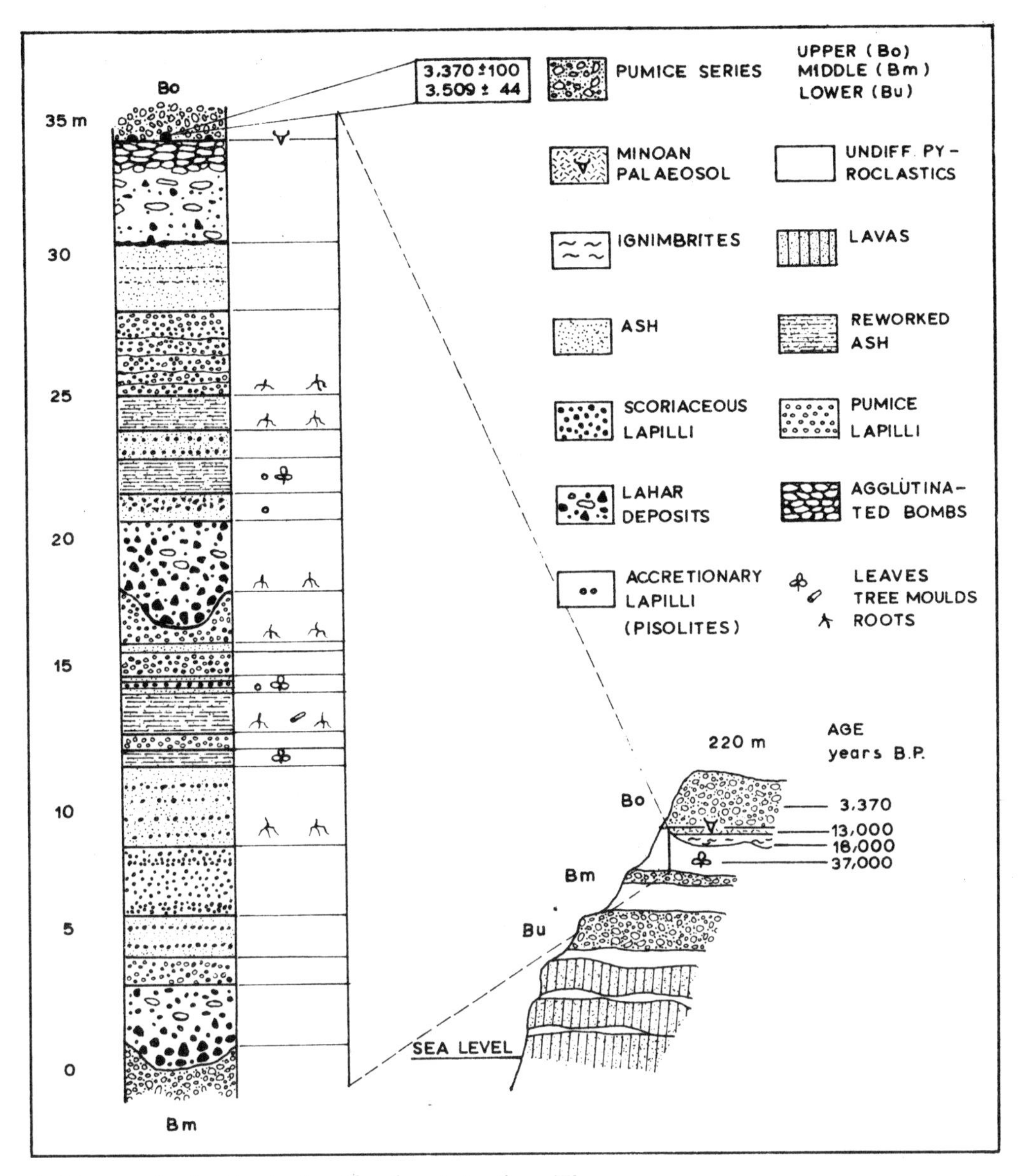

4 Diagram showing the stratigraphy of ancient soils on Thera.

There are also myths which reveal similar relations between the east and west Aegean. For example, the myth of the Telchines, the nine dog-headed Children of the Sea, connects Rhodes with Crete. The legend of Europa further emphasizes these east-west contacts by linking the eastern Mediterranean coast with Crete, Libya, Rhodes and the Greek mainland as well as the Black Sea. There are a host of other myths connected with different parts of the Aegean; it would be impossible to enumerate them all. One stands out, however: the myth of Theseus and the Minotaur, which reflects all the inter-Aegean contacts. The Aegean Sea itself was named after Theseus' father Aegeus. Theseus, his mission to Crete successfully accomplished, set sail for Athens, calling at various islands, including Naxos and Delos in the Cyclades, and, according to another version, Cyprus too.

Thus, for the ancient Greeks, the Aegean was the setting for countless legends, myths and heroic deeds. The islands scattered throughout its waters have their own myths too, immortalizing those distant days before the dawn of history, and Thera is no exception.

The island is referred to, in general, as Thera, but it is also known by other names in the sources. The very ancient name Stronghyle ('the Round One'), that we have already noted, has its parallel in the Italian volcanic island of Stromboli, which was also called Stronghyle by the ancient Greeks. Another name, again mentioned by ancient authors, was Kalliste ('the Most Beautiful'), no doubt referring to the natural beauties of the island. The name Thera itself derives from Theras, son of Autesion, who colonized the island together with his fellow Spartans. Santorini is a relatively recent name–given to the island by the Venetians who ruled the Cyclades during the thirteenth, fourteenth and fifteenth centuries AD–and was apparently taken from a chapel dedicated to St Irene in one of the bays where the Venetians moored their ships.

The volcanic genesis of Thera seems to be evoked in the myth of Euphemus, one of the Argonauts, who, on the instructions of the local god Triton, threw a lump of earth into the sea, north of Lake Tritonis (in Tunisia). This lump of earth was transformed into the island of Thera.

The role of Thera, or Kalliste, in the links between the Greek mainland and the eastern Mediterranean is reflected in the most ancient legends of the Greeks. Libya's and Poseidon's son, Agenor, left Egypt and settled in the land of Canaan, where he married Telephassa who bore him five sons (Cadmus, Phoenix, Cilix, Thasus, Phineus) and one daughter, Europa. Zeus, who fell in love with Europa, disguised himself as a bull, took Europa on his back and swam away from Tyre to the south coast of Crete. There, in a willow-thicket, or under an evergreen plane-tree, he transformed himself into an eagle and ravished Europa, who gave birth to Minos, Rhadamanthys and Sarpedon. After the disappearance of Europa, Agenor, her father, sent his sons in search of their sister, ordering them not to return without her. Not knowing in which direction the bull had gone, they each decided to take a different route. One of them, Cadmus, accompanied by his mother Telephassa, sailed first to Rhodes and then to Thera, where he built a temple to Poseidon. Cadmus moved on to Thrace to continue his search, but before doing so, according to Herodotus, 'either because the land pleased him, or because for some other reason he desired so to do, he left in this island, among other Phoenicians, his own kinsman Membliarus. These dwelt in the island Calliste for eight generations before Theras came from Sparta.'

According to some specialists on ancient Greek mythology Zeus' rape of Europa reflects an early Hellenic occupation of Crete; others see in the story a raid on Phoenicia by Hellenes from Crete. But whatever interpretation is given to the myth, Thera's involvement in it hints at the island's early relations with Crete, the Greek mainland and the eastern Mediterranean.

According to another old legend, Thera had been colonized by Minyans, descendants of the Argonauts, and it was these whom the Dorians from Sparta expelled from the island. This legend reflects Thera's early contacts with the north Aegean regions and the Peloponnese.

2 The Aegean and the Cyclades before the Minoan expansion

The Neolithic background

The Aegean has always played a dual role. On the one hand it separates and isolates, acting as a barrier between those living on the European mainland (Greece) and those on the continent of Asia (Anatolia). On the other hand, as soon as water transport developed this same sea provided the means of communication between groups. Both roles were favourable to the islands scattered throughout the Aegean. Their inhabitants could enjoy security against external attack and at the same time act as middlemen between Greece and Anatolia.

Although on the islands no actual remains of the very remote past have been discovered, there is indirect evidence that the Cyclades were in contact with the Greek mainland as early as the seventh millennium BC. The obsidian (volcanic glass) found in the Mesolithic levels at Franchthi Cave in the Peloponnese has been proved to originate from the Cycladic island of Melos. Melian obsidian has also been found in later, Neolithic, settlements at other places on the Greek mainland, both in the north (Thessaly) and south (Peloponnese) as well as on Crete (Knossos). It cannot, of course, be proved conclusively that the islanders themselves conveyed this volcanic glass from Melos, but it is less plausible to assume that mainlanders were crossing the Aegean at that time. However, from the Late Neolithic settlement of Saliagos near Antiparos (*c.* 4000 BC), as well as from Kephala on Kea (Final Neolithic), comes evidence that these islands were in contact with the Neolithic cultures of continental Greece. The picture in the islands of the north and east Aegean is not quite so clear. In the case of Skyros, for example, it is apparent that the present lack of evidence may be fortuitous and simply due to the limited number of investigations to date.

fig. 3

It is perhaps not surprising that there are no large-scale Neolithic settlements on the Aegean islands. The islands do not possess the extensive fertile plains and rivers which encouraged the growth of fair-sized communities in Anatolia, Thrace, Macedonia, Thessaly, the Pelopponese and Crete.

Early Bronze Age island cultures in the Aegean

Following the pattern set during the Neolithic period, Bronze Age communities in mainland regions around the Aegean developed after 3000 BC in accordance with the agricultural possibilities of their areas. Kingdoms evolved on the rich plains of Anatolia, while lesser (Early Helladic) communities thrived in the more dissected landscapes of mainland Greece. Crete, a fertile island, developed very much along independent lines. The uniform culture that first grew up there in the Early Bronze Age was called Early Minoan by its discoverer, Sir Arthur Evans. Excavating the chief site of Knossos in the 1900s, Evans labelled the entire civilization he was uncovering after Minos, the legendary King of Knossos. Though fanciful, the name has stuck. Middle Minoan culture (2000–1550 BC) was the high-point of Cretan civilization, characterized by great palaces and the centralization of authority under a king.

The small, mainly rocky islands of the Aegean were unsuited to the development of a civilization based on farming and centralized authority. Trade, however, and the islanders' expanding role as middlemen ensured the steady evolution of more complex, integrated societies. Outside Crete two island cultures evolved in the Aegean region during the Early Bronze Age: the Cycladic and the Troadic. The island group of the northeast Aegean (Lemnos, Lesbos, Chios and others) was the cradle of the culture which created the prehistoric cities of Poliochne on Lemnos and Therme on Lesbos, both of which may be considered the earliest urban centres in Europe. Their origins can be traced back as far as the end of the fourth millennium BC. The material culture of these north Aegean communities has been more closely studied than that of any other in the Aegean. Schliemann's excavations at Hissarlik in the Troad after 1871, and the identification of that site as Homer's Troy, meant that the north Aegean culture came to be called Troadic. A major consequence of this has been the unquestioned acceptance of the Troad as the culture's birthplace. The well-stratified site of Hissarlik has certainly been of great significance in the study and classification of the material culture of the north Aegean in the Early Bronze Age, but much of the attention lavished on the site is due to the excitement engendered by its identification with the Homeric city of Troy. Exactly the same problem can be found at Mycenae, which gave its name to the entire Late Bronze Age civilization in the Aegean. It is perhaps significant that both sites–Troy and Mycenae–were first excavated by Heinrich Schliemann in an era when scholarship was pervaded with an air of romanticism.

To return to the north Aegean, it should be observed that the only 'urban' settlements which have been excavated so far are located on the islands (Lemnos and Lesbos) and not on the mainland. The origins of these 'urban' settlements, at least in the case of Poliochne, may be traced back much further than the time of the founding of Troy. Moreover, all the sites investigated to date within the Troad, and identified as belonging to the north Aegean culture, are small-scale and of rather short duration. Even the city of Troy, with its long-lived occupation, is but a small fortified village in comparison with Poliochne or Therme. It would seem, therefore, that during the Early Bronze Age the islands were better suited to the growth of large-scale communities. Among the advantages they shared were good strategic position, enabling them to exercise control over trade; rich fishing grounds in the Dardanelle straits; natural protection from outside assault; and superior experience of the sea in the event of attack.

Thus an autonomous island culture developed in the north Aegean. It managed to maintain its identity for more than a thousand years. In order effectively to control the seaways small settlements–surveillance posts–were established along the shores of the Troad (Troy itself, one may note, is exactly opposite Poliochne). Furthermore, the distribution of the north Aegean culture within the Troad is mainly confined to the coastal areas, gradually disappearing as one proceeds into the hinterland. The mighty cultures of the Anatolian plateau seem to have had little, or no, influence on the Troad. The north Aegean culture fades out to the south, although traces have been found on the islands of Telos and Kalymnos in the Dodecanese. It seems, therefore, that the cradle of the so-called Troadic culture was in the northeast Aegean islands, mainly Lemnos and Lesbos, whence it spread to the east, along the coast of the Troad and to the south, to the northernmost islands of the Dodecanese. Although there is evidence of contact with the coast of Thrace and eastern Macedonia, to date no settlement of purely north Aegean culture has been discovered there–in fact sites in those areas show stronger cultural links with the Balkans.

At the close of the third millennium BC certain changes took place in the north Aegean area which are reflected mainly in the pottery tradition. The so-called Minyan ware, characteristic of most of the Aegean Middle Bronze Age and believed by some to have originated in Troy, came into common use. Whatever caused such changes–the arrival of the Greeks, for example–it is significant that henceforth the north Aegean culture gradually lost its distinctiveness and importance and during the Middle Bronze Age hardly differed from that of mainland Greece.

The Cyclades during the Early and Middle Bronze Age

The second important Early Bronze Age culture in the islands evolved in the southern Aegean, contemporaneously with the development of north Aegean culture. Named after the main chain of islands, the Early Cycladic culture can be traced back as far as the fourth millennium BC and grew out of the indigenous Neolithic culture, as known from the island of Saliagos, near Antiparos, and the site of Kephala on Kea. At this early stage small settlements or nucleated villages were the norm. In the early phases (Early Cycladic I) these settlements were apparently unfortified hamlets of huts scattered throughout the islands. Towards the middle of the third millennium BC, however (about the beginning of Early Cycladic II), an important change seems to have taken place, and most villages moved to hill-tops, protected by fortifications. During this period the influence of the islanders spread to the Greek mainland and Crete, and they may have founded colonies on the coasts of Attica and eastern Crete. It has been suggested that the fortification of the Cycladic settlements reflects clashes between islands and the ascendant power of Crete. If so, these clashes must have taken place over a long period of time. In any event, during the next period, Early

Cycladic III, settlements on the islands moved to the coast, to unfortified sites ensuring safe anchorage. This implies that the menace of the Early Cycladic II period had disappeared. These small coastal 'towns' represent the rudimentary stages of urbanism in the Cyclades, and during the Middle Bronze Age (*c.* 2000–1550 BC) many of them became important harbours. Those known to date are on Melos (Phylakopi), Kea (Ayia Irini), Paros (Paroikia), Thera (Akrotiri) and possibly Naxos (Grotta).

What distinguishes the Cycladic civilization from its counterpart in the north Aegean is its art. Even in the third millennium BC stonecarvers gave form to the snow-white marble of the Cycladic islands. Whatever the meaning of the Cycladic figurines for their owners, whatever they represented, deities or mortals, one thing is certain: they are masterpieces in stone.

The artistic sensitivity of the Cycladic people is manifest in other fields too. In the sphere of two-dimensional art, they must have been the first in the Aegean to produce pictorial motifs. As early as Early Cycladic II human figures, animals and objects (ships, bows etc.) were depicted in rock engravings. Contemporary with this art is the appearance of similar motifs on pottery. Decoration on Early Cycladic II vases includes incised ships, fish and birds. This early preference for pictorial motifs later developed into a definite style and influenced the art of neighbouring cultures. Indeed, birds are the most common theme in Middle and Late Cycladic iconography. Perhaps the great popularity of birds and fish is due to the important part these creatures played in the life of the islanders. Fish, obviously enough, were a basic element in the diet and this may also have been true of birds, especially during the migrating season, since the Cycladic islands are the main stopping off point in the long flight across the Mediterranean. The significance of birds may not just have been dietary, however; their flight over the islands announced the change of seasons, vital information for seafaring and farming peoples.

During the Early Bronze Age contacts were established and maintained between all regions bordering the Aegean. Trade intensified during the Early Cycladic II period. Obsidian from Melos continued to be exported and Early Cycladic II pottery found its way to the north Aegean sites of Poliochne, Troy, Therme and Samos. North Aegean pottery was itself imported into Syros, Naxos, Siphnos and other Cycladic islands. Early Cycladic II contacts with the Greek mainland are demonstrated at sites along the coast of Attica (Palaia Kokkinia, Ayios Kosmas, Brauron, Nea Makri, Marathon) and in the Argolid (Lerna). Evidence of contact with Crete is even stronger, attested by the presence of Early Cycladic II pottery and marble figurines in sites all along the north coast of the island (Archanes, Mochlos, Pseira etc.), as well as the possible Cycladic colony at Ayia Photia in the Seteia region. Further west, Early Cycladic II pottery imports to Kastri are evidence of the islanders' contacts with the island of Kythera.

From the archaeological record there is only evidence of exchange of artefacts between the Cyclades and the north Aegean. Relations with all other regions seem to be one-way: imports from the Cyclades. Perhaps the islanders imported goods of a perishable nature from Crete and the Greek mainland, which would explain why no traces have been left for the archaeologist. This lack of evidence may also be explained by the fact that the islanders, as middlemen, consciously chose what they wished to import and were not interested in bringing pottery vessels from Crete or the mainland since they did not differ appreciably from their own. On the other hand, they probably needed foodstuffs, timber for their houses and boats, and wool and linen for their clothes.

Relations between the Cycladic islanders and those of the north Aegean were somewhat different. The people of the north Aegean were also mariners and traders, and they brought pottery objects to the Cyclades as well as other commodities in the course of trading or fishing expeditions. We do not know the exact nature of the transactions engaged in (barter, ritual exchange), but we do know that imports from the north Aegean were quite quickly adapted and modified to satisfy local tastes and then introduced to the Greek mainland, through the Cyclades. Thus the foundations for the creation of Early Helladic III pottery were laid.

Contacts established by the Cycladic islanders during the Early Bronze Age were continued during the Middle Bronze Age. That links with the Greek mainland were intensified is shown by the presence of abundant Middle Helladic pottery in harbour towns such as Phylakopi (Melos), Paroikia (Paros), Ayia Irini (Kea) and Akrotiri (Thera). This pottery is represented by two categories of vases. The first includes vessels of fine fabric decorated with matt-painted rectilinear motifs, such as the barrel-like pithos, panelled cups, hydriae etc. To the second category belong much rarer vases, the so-called 'leatherware', decorated with either pictorial (birds) or linear motifs. Some ewers are known from Phylakopi and from Akrotiri, while on the mainland they are known from the shaft graves at Mycenae, from Lerna and from Kleidi, near Samikon, in Messenia. The so-called 'Minyan' ware found at Phylakopi, Paroikia and on Kea may be indicative of contacts with the north Aegean, although pottery of this type could also have been imported from Middle Helladic centres. Interestingly, such pottery is entirely absent from Akrotiri. In the aforementioned harbour towns there is the first archaeological evidence of imports from Crete, though it should be noted that this evidence consists only of sherds of Kamares ware, not entire vases. One explanation may be that during the Middle Bronze Age the Cycladic islanders had more vested interests in the Greek mainland than in Crete. Perhaps the Middle Helladic vases found in the Cyclades served also as containers for other goods imported from the mainland. Kamares ware vessels may have been imported as works of art in themselves and not as functional items.

plates 35, 38

These exchanges with both the Greek mainland and Crete suggest that the Cycladic islanders were still in control of the seaways and that both the mainland and Crete accepted this. Thus is explained the absence of fortifications from some Middle Cycladic harbour towns. It is quite likely that the islanders acted as intermediaries in effecting preliminary contacts between Crete and the Greek mainland.

Contact with Middle Minoan civilization drew the Cyclades gradually into Crete's sphere of influence. According to the scholar Arne Furumark, the curvilinear style of pottery decoration, inspired by the Middle Minoan IIIB Kamares style, constitutes the most obvious symptom of this influence. Nevertheless, as this same scholar has admitted, the Cyclades managed to retain their individuality. The Middle Cycladic potters did not slavishly imitate Cretan prototypes and, as Furumark, again, has stated, 'the pottery was still essentially a product of native Cycladic art, its Minoan features being due to impulses that the local potters received from imported Cretan vases.'

The Early and Middle Bronze Age on Thera

Despite the thick deposits of volcanic ash which hinder the archaeologist's attempts to dig down deep into the past of Thera, there is still a substantial body of evidence about Early and Middle Bronze Age cultures on the island. There may have been little systematic excavation beneath the present surface, prior to the work at Akrotiri, but even so at least three Early Cycladic sites have been pinpointed so far. The first of these was discovered in 1840 during the removal of volcanic ash from the Phira quarries: it was probably a cemetery. Among the finds were the two marble figurines now in the Badisches Landesmuseum, Karlsruhe. They are among the finest examples of the islanders' art during Early Cycladic II and their discovery shows that Thera was very much a part of the cultural developments of the third millennium BC. This is confirmed by another, recently surveyed, site on the hill of Archangelos, to the west of the present village of Akrotiri. The hill (without any deposits of pumice or volcanic ash whatsoever) was visited by the author in November 1978 and produced evidence of both Early Cycladic and Late Cycladic I occupation. Among the Early Cycladic sherds are some horizontal handles bearing incised decoration on their upper surface only, which is typical of jars belonging to the Early Cycladic II period. The third Early Cycladic site on Thera is Akrotiri itself. From the deepest levels of the excavation Early Cycladic II and Early Cycladic III pottery fragments are relatively common.

fig. 1

Within Thera's sphere of influence seems to have been the small island to the southwest, Christiana, which has produced the only intact Early Cycladic II vases in the region. This pottery belongs to an advanced phase of Early Cycladic II, characterized by influences from the north Aegean culture, which thus confirms contacts between Thera, its neighbouring island and the north Aegean.

The transition from Early to Middle Bronze Age on Thera was relatively smooth, as it was on the other Cycladic islands. The Early Cycladic II/III coastal settlement at Akrotiri developed into a harbour town, an evolution demonstrated by the important and widely distributed finds. The finds, principally pottery, also constitute strong evidence of the close and continuing contacts between Thera and the Greek mainland throughout the whole of the Middle Bronze Age. Characteristic Middle Helladic vases are found in abundance among the ruins, not only in fragmentary condition but also entire. Though there is evidence of contact with Middle Minoan Crete–in the form of Kamares ware sherds–these links do not seem to have been as strong as those with the Greek mainland.

plates 35, 38

In addition to Akrotiri there is another site on Thera which can be dated to the Middle Cycladic period. It consists of a cluster of graves beneath the thick deposits of Late Minoan tephra and is located in the Karageorghis quarry, almost half-way between Phira and Athinios. Though excavation has not yet been possible, Middle Cycladic vases, in quite good condition, have been turned up by the bulldozer. This limited evidence from Middle Cycladic Thera is sufficient to show that the island was not isolated during the period, but developed and thrived in the same way as the other Cycladic islands, its life being organized around and focussed on the sea.

plate 34

3 The site of Akrotiri

History of the excavation

The present excavation at Akrotiri began in 1967 with the digging of trial trenches at different points along the ravine-pathway leading from the modern village southwards to the sea. Marinatos' choice of site proved to be correct; in just a few hours remains of the buried city started to appear. The next step was to try and determine the extent of the city, to which aim two whole seasons were devoted, in 1967 and 1968.

Marinatos realized from the outset that the Akrotiri excavation was going to be a long-term project which would involve several generations of archaeologists. In these early years a great deal of attention was therefore paid to the organization of proper facilities for the dig. Substantial workshops and laboratories were built for the storage, repair, treatment and examination of the finds. Accommodation for the staff was also constructed. Special problems were presented by the burial of the site beneath a thick mantle of volcanic debris and a number of different methods of excavation were tried out. Marinatos had observed almost from the start that the houses were preserved to a height of more than one storey and he thought long and hard about the best method of excavating them. To begin with he experimented by tunnelling in the layers of pumice and volcanic ash. In this way he hoped to enter the houses through their doors, keeping them buried underground so as to create a dramatic 'living' museum whilst retaining the vineyards above. This ambitious and somewhat romantic plan had to be abandoned in haste and even Marinatos, who had conceived and publicized it, ceased to mention it after the third excavation season. Tunnelling was abandoned for a number of reasons. First of all, robbed of the supporting material around them, the houses were in great danger of collapse. Secondly, the tunnels themselves were a hazard, since the volcanic ash tended to dry out on exposure to air and become powdery and structurally unsound. Thirdly, it was in any case impossible to enter through the house doors because the floors of the upper storeys, which had partially collapsed, would then have caved in completely. Finally, tunnelling is most unscientific; there is complete disregard for stratigraphy and sequence and finds are condemned to destruction by the speedy pick.

To protect the excavated remains from erosion a roof was erected over the site supported on Dexion pillars. The ancient buildings had been constructed of plate 10 rubble and clay reinforced with timber, but in 3,500 years the timber had disintegrated and the clay had crumbled, so that without the protective roof the buildings might have collapsed after the lightest shower of rain. The Dexion system has many advantages. It is quick to erect and can be expanded in any direction, so that newly exposed ruins in any part of the site can be covered without delay. It also does away with the need for solid side walls, which would obstruct the view of the site. Most important of all, the freestanding metal pillars can be placed up to 12 m apart, which gives the excavator enough flexibility to be able to position the pillars where they will cause least damage to the site. At Akrotiri pits for the pillars were dug right down to bedrock and the pillars inserted in them if no architectural remains came to light. Since the pits were methodically excavated, they also provided useful information about the stratigraphy and history of the site.

The total disintegration of all kinds of timberwork posed other problems, particularly where buildings were preserved to a height of two and three storeys. The wooden wall reinforcements and door- and window-frames had left only negative impressions in the surrounding pumice, thus jeopardizing the stability of the buildings. It was therefore necessary to replace the missing timber with some other material. Concrete was eventually chosen because of its strength, its ability to adhere to the existing masonry and its fluidity, which allowed it to be poured into holes and assume the shape of the missing wood.

plates 13–15

Once these major problems had been dealt with–and tunnelling had been abandoned–excavation proceeded in the classical way, that is, by gradual removal of layers from top to bottom. The whole site had been mapped and photographed from the air before excavations began. Marinatos, however, did not feel it necessary to work from a conventional grid of squares during the actual digging, and finds and features were originally plotted in relation to the well-preserved walls. Unfortunately this now means it is impossible to reconstruct the exact relationship of some of the buildings to the site overall before they were excavated. Today a grid is being used; it is applied systematically so that, together with help from the stratigraphical plans, finds can be associated with one another as well as with the various rooms of a building.

fig. 5

Ten buildings have been explored–though not completely–so far. In addition, at least another seven are known to lie under the roofed area. Marinatos gave each building a particular name, though not using a consistent system. Sometimes the buildings are designated by letters of the Greek alphabet (Buildings Alpha, Beta, Gamma and Delta), and the individual rooms by arabic numerals (Room Delta 2, for example, means Room number 2 of Building Delta). In other cases the name of the building reflects its method of construction–one with walls made of dressed stone is called Xesté, which in Greek means 'ashlar'. So Building Delta, because of its ashlar north façade, has also been called Xesté 1, and other buildings have been called Xesté 2, Xesté 3 and Xesté 4. Here again individual rooms are designated by arabic numerals (e.g. Xesté 3, Room 5). The House of the Ladies, on the other hand, was named after the wall-painting showing women in Minoan dress which was discovered in one of its rooms. Finally, the West House was so called because at the time of its discovery it was the westernmost building of the site (arabic numerals are again used to identify each individual room).

One of the main characteristics of the site is the large number of finds. A single room may produce several hundred items consisting of pottery, stone vases, stone tools and implements, minor objects and, occasionally, negatives of broken pieces of furniture from which casts can be obtained. Thus the yield each season comprises thousands of objects, all of which have to be cleaned, mended, restored, catalogued, photographed and often drawn. To try and ensure that nothing is missed during the excavation, sieving has been used selectively. Although a permanent water-sieving installation was constructed in 1976, dry-sieving has been found generally to be adequate. Water-sieving is slow, the plant remains it produces are often duplicated by remains in jars, and objects of any size are in fact recovered more effectively by dry-sieving.

Even more specialized techniques were required when it was discovered early on in the excavation that the site contained a large number of miraculously preserved wall-paintings. Fortunately Greece has at its disposal a veritable army of experts in the restoration and removal of Byzantine frescoes, and their skills were applied most successfully to the Theran paintings. Tassos Margaritoff, one of the chief restorers of Byzantine icons and wall-paintings in Greece, is general supervisor of the Akrotiri operation. His chief collaborator, Stamatis Perrakis, is head of the team on the spot, and some of his best pupils, including Iakovos Michaelides, Stavros Angelides and Panayiotis Dritsas, now form the core of a true school of restorers specializing in the conservation of the Theran wall-paintings. As a result, today there are a dozen people, with several years' experience, who are exclusively employed on this major project.

The first fragments of wall-painting were found in 1968 in Sector Alpha (then called Arvaniti 1), and included the head of an African, the head of a blue monkey and some large flying blue birds. Despite their fragmentary condition these pieces revealed that a great art had flourished at Akrotiri and justified Marinatos' enthusiasm–he went so far as to see in these fragments a Greek myth and wrote on 20 September 1968 in his daybook: 'I begin to wonder if it is "Orpheus" or "Thamyris" with a lyre having in front of him all the birds of the forest. . . .'

But this was only the beginning. The discovery, in 1969, of the wall-painting of the 'Blue Monkeys' in Room Beta 6 (then Bronos 2) increased the general excitement still further. The rocky landscape on which the monkeys were climbing was very similar to the volcanic rocks near the site. In 1970 the excavation of the wall-paintings reached its emotional climax with the uncovery of the 'Spring Fresco' in Room Delta 2, the first, and so far the only, wall-painting to be found perfectly preserved and still standing in its original position. The slow process of removing the volcanic ash with a brush and the gradual revelation, inch by inch, of this magnificent work of art kept us in a state of continuous

plate IX

plate III

Colour plates (pages 33–40)

I View towards the east, showing the roofed-in excavation area at ancient Akrotiri in the centre of the picture.

II Triangle Square seen from the south, with the West House on the left and Building Complex Delta on the right.

III The 'Spring Fresco' on the walls of Room Delta 2, after restoration. A detail of the swallows and lilies in this rocky landscape can be seen in plate 28.

IV The 'Boxing Children' fresco from the south wall of Room Beta 1. The position of this fresco in the room is shown in plate 26.

V Specialists cleaning a newly restored wall-painting (shown upside down) from Xesté 3.

VI Fresco from the north wall of a corridor in the House of the Ladies. A woman with bared breasts and Minoan-style dress leans towards another figure, probably seated, of which only part of the dress has survived. This composition stood opposite a similar one shown in plate 27.

VII Papyruses are depicted clustered together on the western walls of Room 1 in the House of Ladies.

VIII The 'Antelopes' fresco from the west wall of Room Beta 1. See also plate 26.

IX Part of the frieze of eight blue monkeys in a rocky landscape which apparently covered at least two walls in Room Beta 6.

X The most important fresco from Akrotiri: the 'Flotilla' frieze from the south wall of Room 5 in the West House. The general theme seems to be the voyage of a flotilla from one harbour town and its arrival at another. See also figs 12, 20 and 21.

XI One of the eight enigmatic devices depicted on the walls of Room 4 in the West House. Upright poles topped by Egyptian lilies support decorated screens. Marinatos originally thought they might be 'banners', but later decided they were 'cabins'. A more recent theory, however, sees them as litters or palanquins.

XII The well-preserved 'Fisherman' fresco from the north wall of Room 5 in the West House. Cf. fig. 12.

XIII Fresco of the 'Young Priestess' from the northeast corner of Room 4 in the West House. She holds a glowing brazier and seems to sprinkle it with incense.

XIV The so-called 'Sea Battle' fresco, one of two groups of fragments from the north wall of Room 5 in the West House. Three different scenes are depicted one above the other, perhaps to indicate perspective. In the foreground three ships are shown either side of drowning warriors, the victims of a sea battle or shipwreck. Above this five warriors march in single file to the right, away from a single-storey building. At the top of the fresco shepherds drive a flock of sheep into a pen or circular enclosure – possibly the artist wished to convey the idea of a peaceful country scene about to be disrupted by the marching soldiers below. Cf. fig. 12.

XV On the east wall of Room 5 in the West House stood this fresco of a river landscape. Wild beasts pursue each other amidst palm trees and other exotic vegetation along the banks of a meandering river. For a detail, see plate 29.

I

II

IV

V

VI

VII

VIII

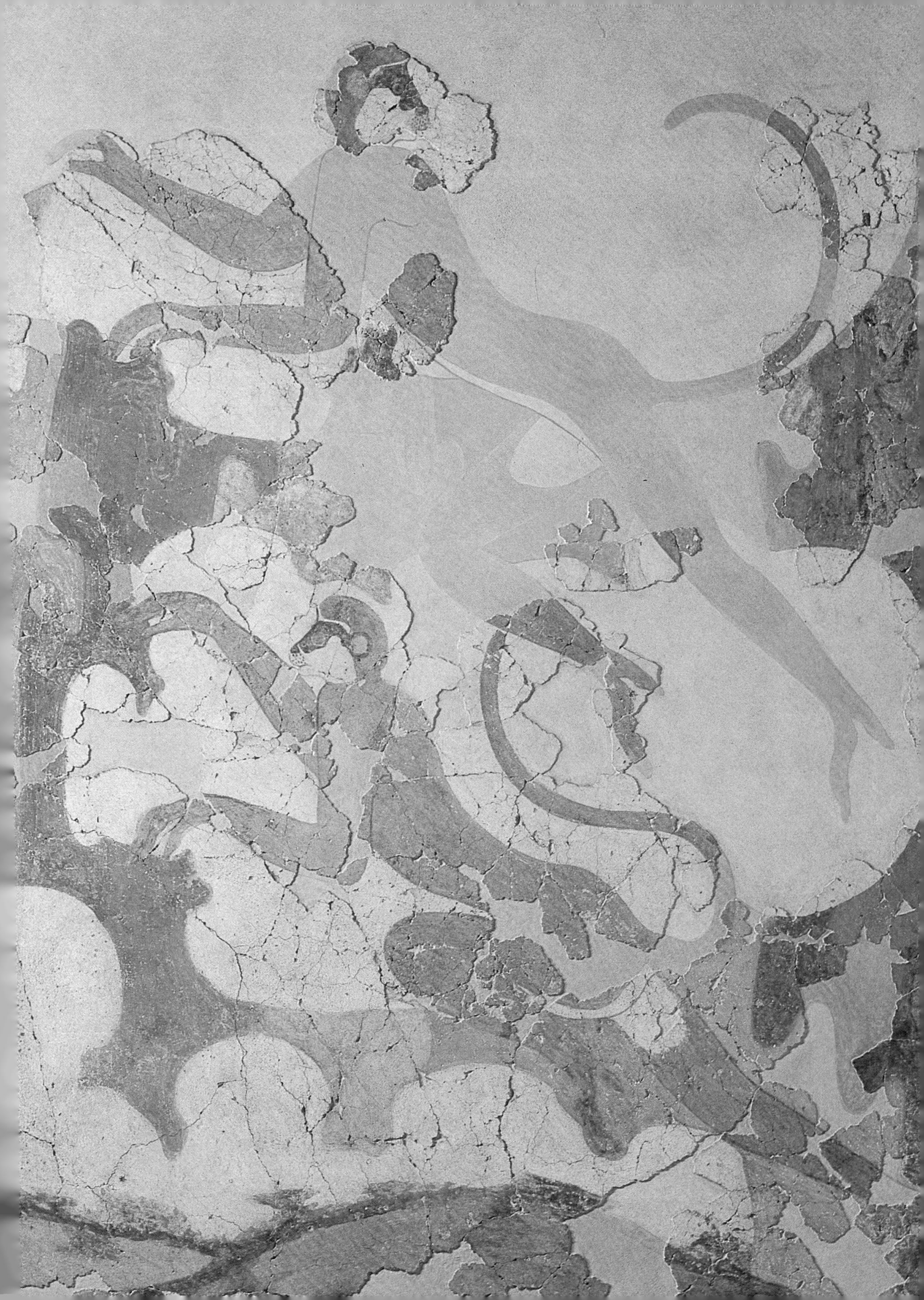

X

XI

XII

XIII

XIV

XV

excitement for weeks. The supporting wall was not in perfect condition, so the painting had to be removed immediately. Our experts–Perrakis and his team–were quite calm. Their experience in removing large Byzantine frescoes had given them the requisite confidence. But the prehistorians, who were confronted with such a problem for the first time, could not hide their anxiety. Even Marinatos, who normally had no hesitation in making quick decisions, was worried and decided to organize an on-the-spot meeting of the three most eminent Greek experts, Tassos Margaritoff, Stavros Baltoyiannis and Photis Zachariou. The meeting lasted two days. In the end, the following procedure was adopted. The entire wall-painting was covered with gauze to prevent it from falling. On top of the gauze, stronger and heavier material was then stuck, and on top of that, a series of strong bands positioned vertically at short intervals (*c.* 30cm). The bands started from the bottom of the wall and rose to about 1 m above it. Their free end (at the top) was fastened to a beam running parallel to and above the painting. In this way the entire surface of the wall was suspended from the beam. Once the painting had been prevented from collapsing, the process of removal began. A polystyrene mould of the wall was made which created a bed for the fresco. Next, Perrakis started to work at the back of the plaster with 2-m-long steel needles–invented for the occasion–trying to disconnect the fresco from the wall, until eventually the entire painting was literally suspended from the beam. Slowly and cautiously the beam, the mould and the plaster were lowered. The wall-painting was now in a horizontal position, resting on its mould face downwards, and another mould was made for its back. The sandwich thus created was then safely transported to the laboratory for further treatment.

Rescuing the 'Spring Fresco' was a delicate operation, and provided invaluable experience for the archaeologists and restorers. A few other paintings (the 'Fisherman' from the West House and a lady from the House of the Ladies) have been found standing, though detached from the wall. But the great majority of the frescoes were discovered in fragments, which requires a slightly different technique of excavation. Here it is essential to apply the grid system rigorously, so that the coordinates of each fragment within each grid-square can be noted and the fragment drawn *in situ.* Only by such detailed and meticulous recording can the original fresco be accurately reconstructed in the laboratory. Once these records have been made the fragment is impregnated with acetone to remove moisture. It is then consolidated, both the plaster and the paint, in various stages with different dilutions of epoxy resin in acetone. A piece of gauze is spread over the exposed surface of the fragment and stuck to it with a more concentrated solution of this same adhesive. When it has dried the gauze-and-fresco fragment is removed to the laboratory, where it undergoes a lengthy process of restoration. The gauze is removed, the fragment cleaned and then with luck and skill it is fitted into the jigsaw puzzle that is the whole fresco. At a later stage gaps between the fragments are filled in judiciously and the complete wall-painting is enclosed within a frame before final overall restoration. Thus by the diligent pursuit of a systematic method of recovery the artistic masterpieces of thirty-five centuries ago can be restored to something like their original splendour.

Akrotiri before Late Cycladic I

The earliest evidence of habitation at Akrotiri comes from the pits dug down to bedrock for the supporting pillars of the roof. In the lower deposits pottery fragments of the Early Cycladic II and III periods have been found in quite large numbers. Vase forms which can be readily reconstructed from these sherds belong to the advanced phases of the EC II and EC III periods. Some of the pottery is of the variant indicative of contacts with the north Aegean, black and brown burnished ware. However, so far no evidence has been found which could prove similar contacts between Akrotiri and Crete or the Greek mainland.

Certain subterranean structures dug in the relatively soft volcanic rock seem to be connected with the Early Cycladic pottery. It has proved difficult to investigate these structures because of the superimposed buildings. It would seem, however, that they are rock-cut chambers, some of which were used secondarily even in Late Cycladic times.

Remains of the Middle Cycladic period are more copious and better preserved. They are also widely distributed throughout the site, indicating the increased importance and extent of the settlement during the Middle Bronze Age (*c.* 2000–1550 BC). The Middle Cycladic pottery of Akrotiri shares the characteristics known from other islands, in particular those of the pottery from Phylakopi and Paros. Among the commonest recognizable forms are the 'Cycladic' bowl (with incurved rim), the oil lamp and an early type of breasted ewer. The vases are usually of fine fabric, and their matt-painted dark-on-light decoration consists of geometric (mainly curvilinear) and pictorial motifs. Among the latter, birds of various kinds predominate.

Matt-painted Middle Helladic pottery seems to have been imported at Akrotiri in considerable quantities, indicating close contact with mainland Greece at this time. The vases are often found intact and are quite sizeable, for instance the barrel-like jar, the hydria and the amphora in the form of a compressed sphere. Middle Helladic panelled cups are not unusual; their popularity is confirmed by the large number of local imitations. Middle Helladic decoration mainly comprises linear geometric patterns. Besides this category there are also some vases of so-called 'leatherware', further proof of close links with the Greek mainland.

plates 35, 38

Unlike the other known Middle Cycladic sites (Phylakopi, Ayia Irini, Paroikia), vases of so-called 'Minyan' ware are totally lacking from Akrotiri. There has been much scholarly debate about the original provenance of this type of pottery, typical of the Aegean Middle Bronze Age. Some scholars consider it to be a product of the north Aegean culture, while others favour a Helladic centre.

Its absence from Akrotiri, which apparently kept in close touch with Middle Helladic Greece, would suggest that Minyan ware was not in fact produced on the Greek mainland.

Akrotiri's lack of contact with the north Aegean seems to have been counterbalanced by the development of close relations with Crete. For the first time Middle Minoan Cretan imports appear, in the form of small Kamares-style cups. Nevertheless, if frequency of imported pottery is regarded as an indicator of degree of contact, then Middle Cycladic Akrotiri kept much more closely in touch with mainland Greece than with Crete. This is only to be expected bearing in mind the long tradition of contact between the mainland and the Cyclades; Crete's intervention in Aegean affairs seems to have been initiated as late as the Middle Minoan period.

In addition to pottery, other Middle Cycladic artefacts testify to the importance of the settlement during this period. Lapidary art, for instance, which in the rest of the Cyclades was most refined and advanced during the Early Bronze Age, is much in evidence in Middle Cycladic Akrotiri. A large raw piece of Melian obsidian found in a Middle Cycladic context suggests that this material must have been worked in local workshops. Since there is no native marble on Thera the stone-carvers used other materials, particularly the characteristic grey-black lava. Out of this was made the largest stone vessel known from the entire prehistoric Aegean. It is a barrel-shaped pithos which was found in a Middle Cycladic context, east of Delta 3. Its shape, in particular its broad vertical strap handles, inset base of neck and solid vertical lugs at the junction of neck and body, are features observed on Early Cycladic pithoi, which seemingly inspired the Theran artisan. A stool of the same stone, and probably by the same craftsman, was found alongside this pithos. It is the only known piece of Middle Cycladic furniture.

fig. 17

Architectural remains of the Middle Cycladic period are more numerous and better preserved than those of the Early Cycladic. Some of the buildings of the subsequent Late Cycladic period are actually built on top of, or are modifications of, earlier buildings. The best example of this is Building Complex Delta, Room 16 of which was built on to pre-existing walls. In other places, particularly open spaces such as the square to the south of Mill House Delta 15 and to the east of Delta 3, foundations of Middle Cycladic buildings can be observed. From these traces it may be inferred that the town plan in Middle Cycladic times was more or less the same as that in Late Cycladic times, and only where the Late Cycladic architects required more space for a square or street were existing buildings cleared away.

From the archaeological record it is apparent that the transition from Middle to Late Cycladic civilization at Akrotiri was marked by a general destruction. Quite thick destruction levels are found throughout the excavated area, including amongst their debris large quantities of broken pottery. Both Middle and Late Cycladic ceramics occur in almost equal proportion, which suggests that the destruction took place at a time when Middle Cycladic pottery, although still in common use, was beginning to give way to the new style introduced from Crete (Late Minoan IA). From this evidence it can be deduced that the destruction must have occurred about 1550 BC.

Considering the fact that some of the Late Cycladic buildings are additions to, or modifications of, severely damaged Middle Cycladic houses, it may be concluded that the overall destruction of Middle Cycladic Akrotiri was due to an earthquake. Whether the epicentre of the earthquake was Thera itself we do not know. It should be noted, however, that similar serious destructions, at almost the same time, are observed in the palaces of Crete, in Phylakopi on Melos, Kastri on Kythera and Ayia Irini on Kea. Though also attributed to earthquakes, these destructions do not seem to have affected life in these places, or to have caused any disruption or retardation in cultural and economic progress. On the contrary, a subsequent quick recovery and widespread rebuilding is attested. So, even if the epicentre of the earthquake was not on Thera, it cannot have been very far away.

The destruction of Middle Cycladic Akrotiri gave the inhabitants an opportunity to rebuild their houses in a more luxurious and magnificent manner, as is evident from the recent excavations. This implies that Middle Cycladic Akrotiri was a thriving community at the time of the disaster. Taking into account the evidence of foreign contacts, it may be suggested that the people of Akrotiri were involved in mercantile marine activities and perhaps handled the trade between the Greek mainland and Crete.

4 The Late Cycladic city of Akrotiri

Extent

As we have seen, the settlement of Akrotiri did not suddenly appear from nowhere during the Late Bronze Age. It followed the course of cultural development observed throughout the Cyclades from at least the middle of the third millennium BC (i.e. the middle of the Early Cycladic period). The distribution of both Early and Middle Cycladic pottery within the excavated area shows that the settlements which pre-dated the Late Cycladic I city were quite important and extensive. This is particularly true of the Middle Cycladic settlement, which merits description as a town. Its size, location and geographical situation encouraged the development of a large coastal trading-station, characteristic of the Middle Bronze Age. In about 1550 BC this thriving conurbation was destroyed, most probably by an earthquake, only to be rebuilt anew on a grander scale as the Late Cycladic I houses indicate. In the course of this rebuilding some damaged houses were refurbished, some added to, others demolished. On the whole, however, the Late Cycladic I builders were remarkably faithful to the old plan of the settlement.

The size of the Late Cycladic I city–for as we shall see it can be classed as such–must have been considerable by the standards of the time. Although various scientific techniques have been applied in an attempt to locate its extremities, these have failed and its limits must be deduced from circumstantial evidence. So far an area of over 10,000 square metres has been uncovered and there is no sign at any point that the outskirts of the settlement have been reached. Of the sites known from the periphery of the excavation, the recently located ruins at Balos and in the Mavromatis quarry may have been suburbs of the city. They are more than a kilometre from the site. The site excavated by Zahn in the Potamos Valley is only about 600 m away and may also have been part of the city. This is further hinted at by the fact that the ground between the excavation and the Potamos Valley does not follow the natural southward slope, although of the same volcanic ash, but rises towards the sea, thus creating a concave plateau inland. The plateau can be explained if one supposes that the ground has subsided over collapsed multi-storey houses. Assuming this interpretation is correct, the area of the city including the concave plateau could have been of the order of 200,000 square metres. As to the number of inhabitants, there must have been several thousand if one takes into account the size and number of multi-storey residences unearthed to date.

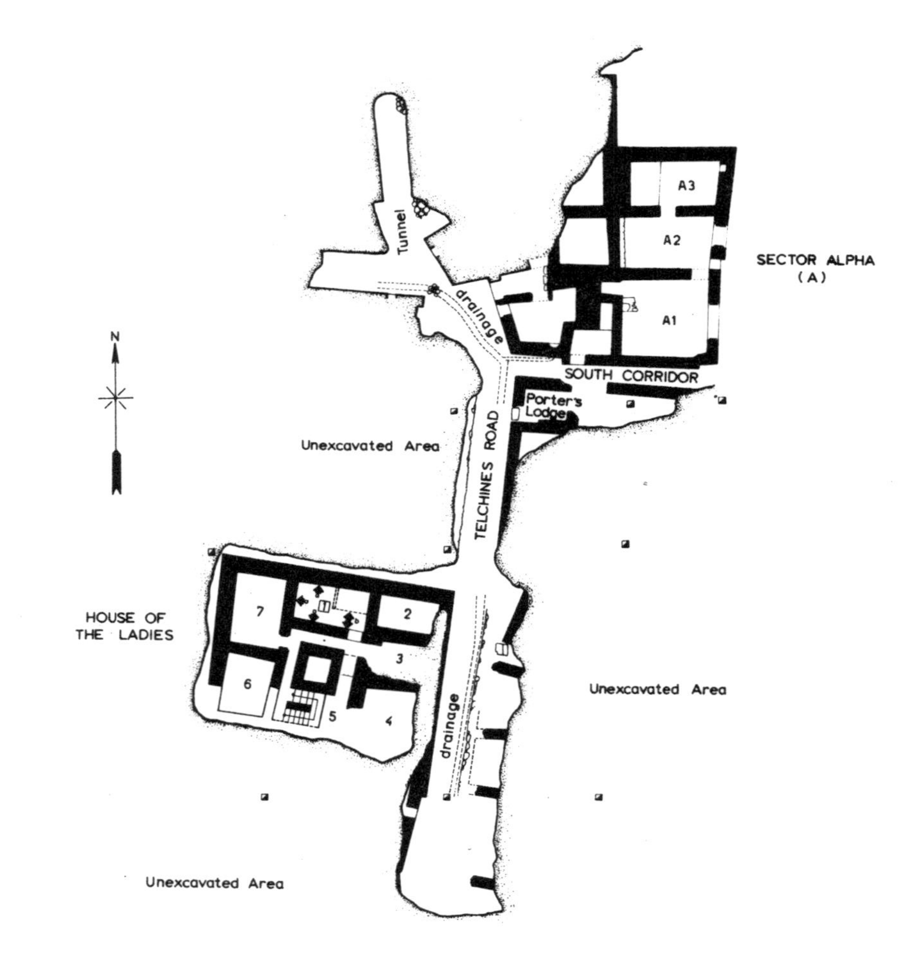

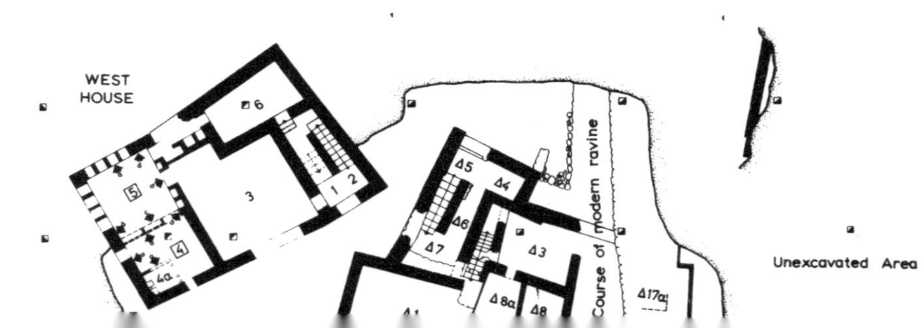

5 *Plan of the excavated buildings at ancient Akrotiri (those with frescoes are listed below). For details of the buildings see figs 6–11.*

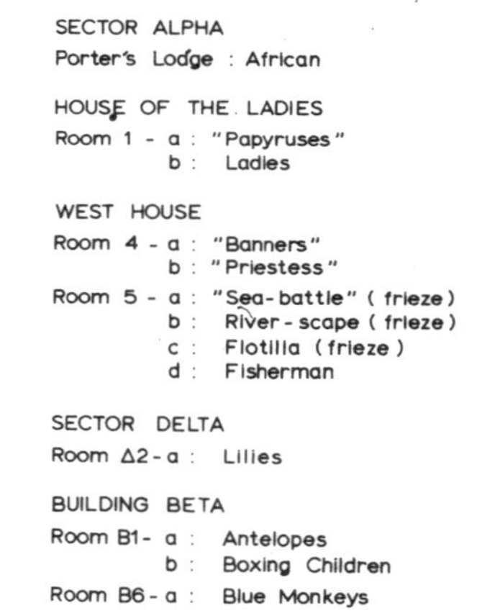

SECTOR ALPHA
Porter's Lodge : African

HOUSE OF THE LADIES
Room 1 - a : "Papyruses"
b : Ladies

WEST HOUSE
Room 4 - a : "Banners"
b : "Priestess"
Room 5 - a : "Sea-battle" (frieze)
b : River-scape (frieze)
c : Flotilla (frieze)
d : Fisherman

SECTOR DELTA
Room Δ2 - a : Lilies

BUILDING BETA
Room B1 - a : Antelopes
b : Boxing Children
Room B6 - a : Blue Monkeys

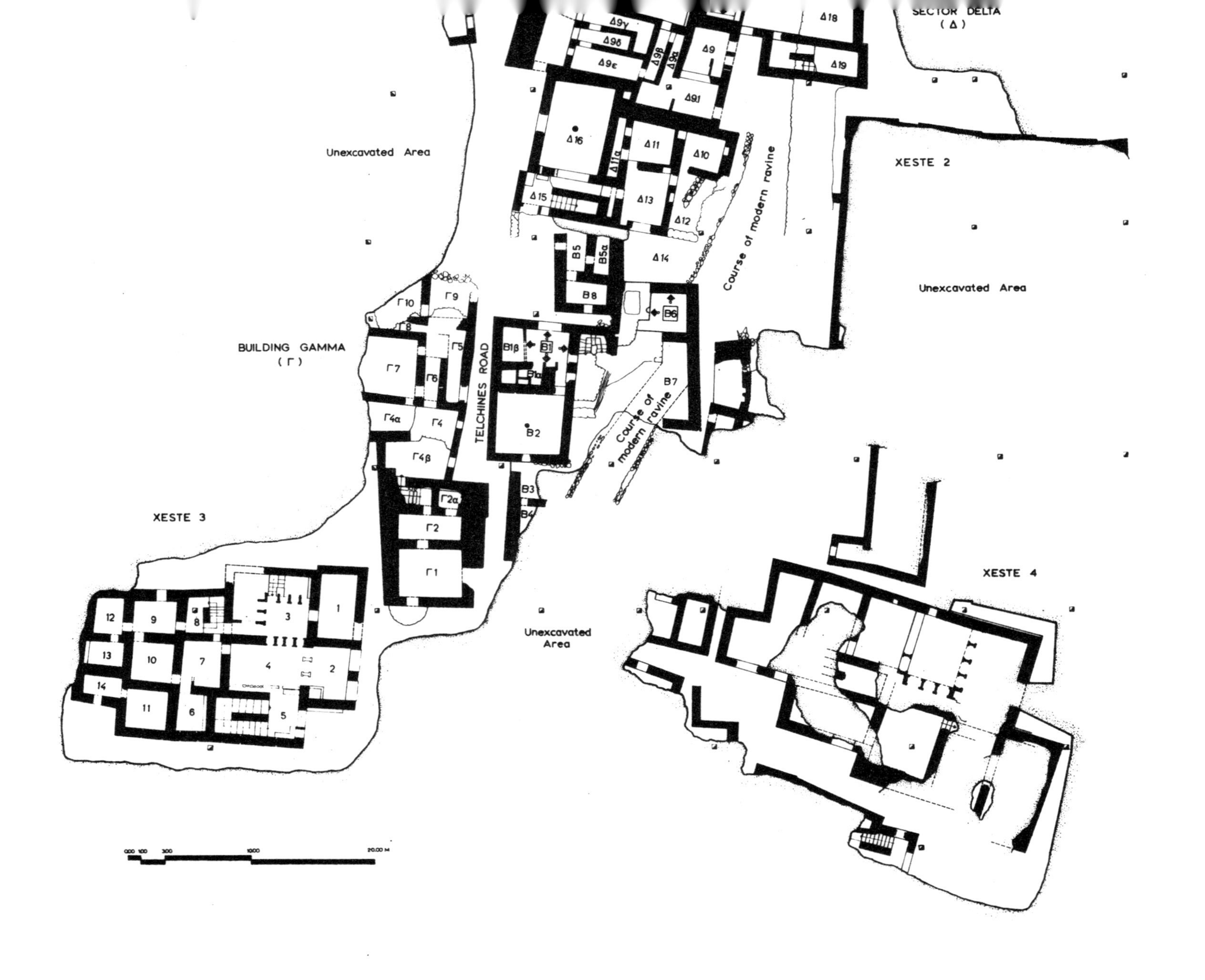
SECTOR DELTA
(Δ)
XESTE 2
Unexcavated Area
Course of modern ravine
Unexcavated Area
BUILDING GAMMA
(Γ)
TELCHINES ROAD
Course of modern ravine
XESTE 3
Unexcavated Area
XESTE 4
20.00 M

fig. 5 Only ten buildings have been uncovered so far, and not one has been fully explored. *Building Alpha* had at least two storeys, as a spare stone column base found in the debris of Room Alpha 1 and the preserved floor of the upper storey in its western wing demonstrate. The ground floor of the eastern wing has been fully explored and consists of Rooms Alpha 1, Alpha 2 and Alpha 3, which were literally packed with jars and other pottery vessels. A low quadrilateral hearth was found in Room Alpha 1 and next to it a small stone basin sunk into the floor. Of the western wing only one room has been investigated, housing a mill installation as well as a lavatory. The ground floors of the east and west wings had separate entrances, but it seems that they interconnected in the upper storeys, access to which could have been through the entrance to the west wing.

At its southernmost end the only street to have been uncovered, running from north to south, was flanked by Building Beta to the east and Building Gamma to the west. Because stone tools (hammers, anvils) were discovered in Building Gamma Marinatos named the street Telchines Road, after the sea monsters who, according to one version of the myth, taught men the arts.

fig. 9 *Building Beta* has been severely damaged by a modern ravine and has only partly been explored. It was a two-storey building consisting of at least eight rooms at ground level. In two of these rooms were found storage jars (Beta 1) and cooking pots (Beta 2). Two or more rooms in the upper storey (Rooms 1 and 6) were decorated with wall-paintings. plates IV, VIII, IX

fig. 5 Opposite Building Beta to the west lies *Building Gamma,* of which only three rooms have really been investigated. From the remains of a staircase and some walls it has become clear that here again there must have been two storeys.

Adjacent to Building Beta to the north is the enormous complex known as *Building Delta*. *fig. 10* Excavation of this is more-or-less complete, but several problems remain to be solved. It appears that the complex is the result of at least five successive additions to an original core. Each addition was provided with its own entrance, but some rooms in the upper storeys were interlinked. There were at least two storeys and evidence of a third has been found at the northernmost end. At ground-floor level Building Delta comprises more than twenty rooms. A stone-built quadrilateral hearth has been found in Room Delta la. plate III Room Delta 2 contained the magnificent wall-painting of the lilies, Room Delta 9 was packed with pottery and Room Delta 16 probably constituted a shop for pottery, stone vases and other commodities.

fig. 11 The *House of the Ladies,* north of Building Delta, was at least three-storeyed. Only three rooms have been fully excavated and therefore even the outline of the building is still unknown. plate VI Besides the wall-paintings of the ladies and the papyrus plants, plate VII the excavated rooms have produced large quantities of pottery and stone vases.

fig. 6 The *West House,* between the House of the Ladies and Building Delta, has been almost fully investigated. Its west wing was two-storeyed but the staircase at its east end suggests the existence of a third storey or an attic there. Six major rooms have been uncovered, producing the usual mass of pottery and stone ves-

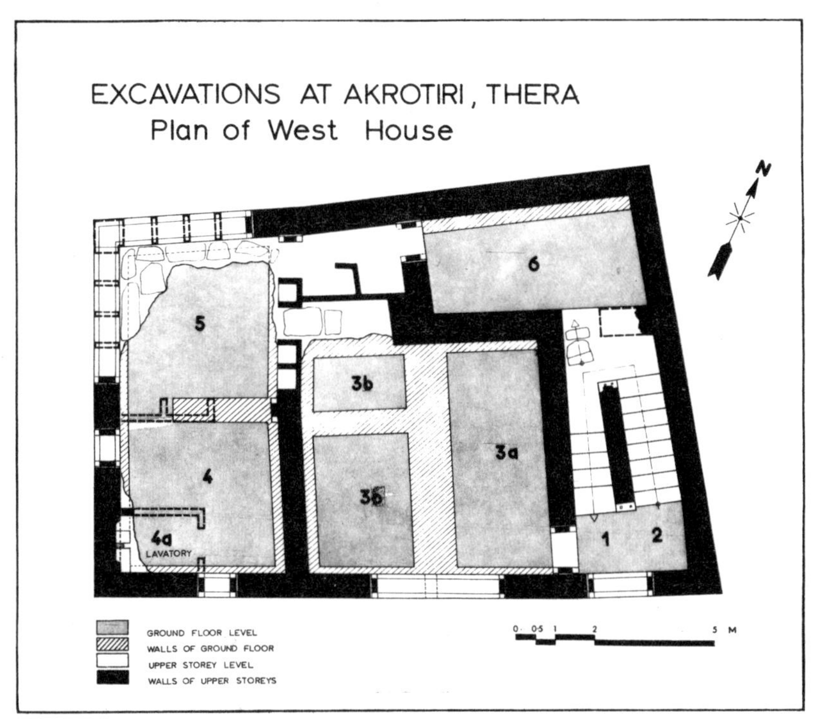

6 Ground plan of the West House.

sels. The upper storey of the west wing was decorated with magnificent wall-paintings: Room 4 produced the 'banners' and the 'Young Priestess' and Room 5 contained the two 'Fishermen' panels and the friezes with the miniature paintings. The southwest corner, still in the upper storey, was occupied by the superb bathroom and toilet installation (Room 4a).

plates XI, XIII
plates XII, XIV, XV

Xesté 2, east of Building Delta, was a three-storey building on the evidence of its north façade, the only part of the building yet uncovered. This façade provides a very good example of combined stone and timberwork construction.

fig. 5

Xesté 3, southwest of Building Gamma, has been investigated quite thoroughly, except for the ground floor of a few rooms. It is a rather large building consisting of at least fourteen rooms at ground level. One of its main characteristics is the extensive use of the pier-and-door arrangement between ground-floor rooms. This, together with the vast quantity of wall-paintings (still incompletely restored) and the 'lustral basin' (so far unique at Akrotiri), lead one to think in terms of a public building. Two of the storeys are quite well preserved, but in the north wing a staircase suggests a third floor, at least in that section.

fig. 7

Xesté 4, southeast of Building Beta, remains entirely unexplored. Only its outline has been uncovered, showing that the whole building–quite extensive–was lined with ashlar masonry. Even the floor-slabs of the third storey are still preserved in their original position.

fig. 5

Town plan and architecture

The general plan of the city, so far as it is known from excavation, in many respects resembles that of the present-day villages of Thera. The city is traversed by narrow, winding streets, just like the modern villages. In the prehistoric site, however, the streets delineate separate mansions or building complexes, while in the villages they segregate insulae of houses. This is the picture in the sector of the city which has been revealed. Whether this town plan arose haphazardly or systematically we do not know. But the morphological similarities between the ancient and modern layouts seem to be due to the influence of similar problems. Streets are geared to the needs of a society without vehicles, and are wide enough for two loaded donkeys or pack animals to pass one another. The winding course of the streets may have been a deliberate attempt to check violent gusts of wind or to prevent the undermining of house foundations by floods during torrential rain. Although the irregular shape of some of the house plots may have contributed to the zigzag nature of the streets, in several instances buildings have been deliberately constructed with denticulated façades. Quite often the open space between two or three buildings forms a kind of square from which other streets radiate, an ideal arrangement for quick escape from an enemy. These tortuous alleys and odd-shaped squares give the settlement very much the appearance of a medieval town.

fig. 5

plate 13

plate II

As a rule, the streets were paved with sizeable stones, more-or-less flat on their upper surface. The city sewers ran beneath these flagstones, and consisted of narrow stone-lined ditches covered with slabs. The sewers were connected to pits beneath the streets which received effluent from domestic lavatories via clay pipes incorporated in house walls.

Excavation of the north section of the Telchines Road, the paved surface of which was severely damaged by torrential rain in modern times, has revealed much of the drainage system in that street. It ran parallel to the unexcavated building east of the House of the Ladies, and the east wall of the sewer actually formed the west wall of that building.

plate 8

The best-preserved example of a lavatory was uncovered in the southwest corner of the West House. It consists of a stone-built seat divided into two. From the base of these two parts and between them runs the clay pipe linking up with the sewers beneath the street. The discovery of this elaborate sewage and drainage system demonstrates the high standard of civilization achieved at the time in the Aegean. Not until several millennia later was this level reached in western Europe.

plates 17, 18

There is no standard house-plan at Akrotiri. Orientation, size and internal arrangement seem to have been a matter of personal choice to meet individual requirements. There are, however, some general functional principles applicable to almost all the buildings. For example, the doorway of the house was invariably flanked by a window–this is perhaps the origin of the Greek word for window, *parathyron* (literally, 'beside the door'). This arrangement ensured that

plates 14, 15

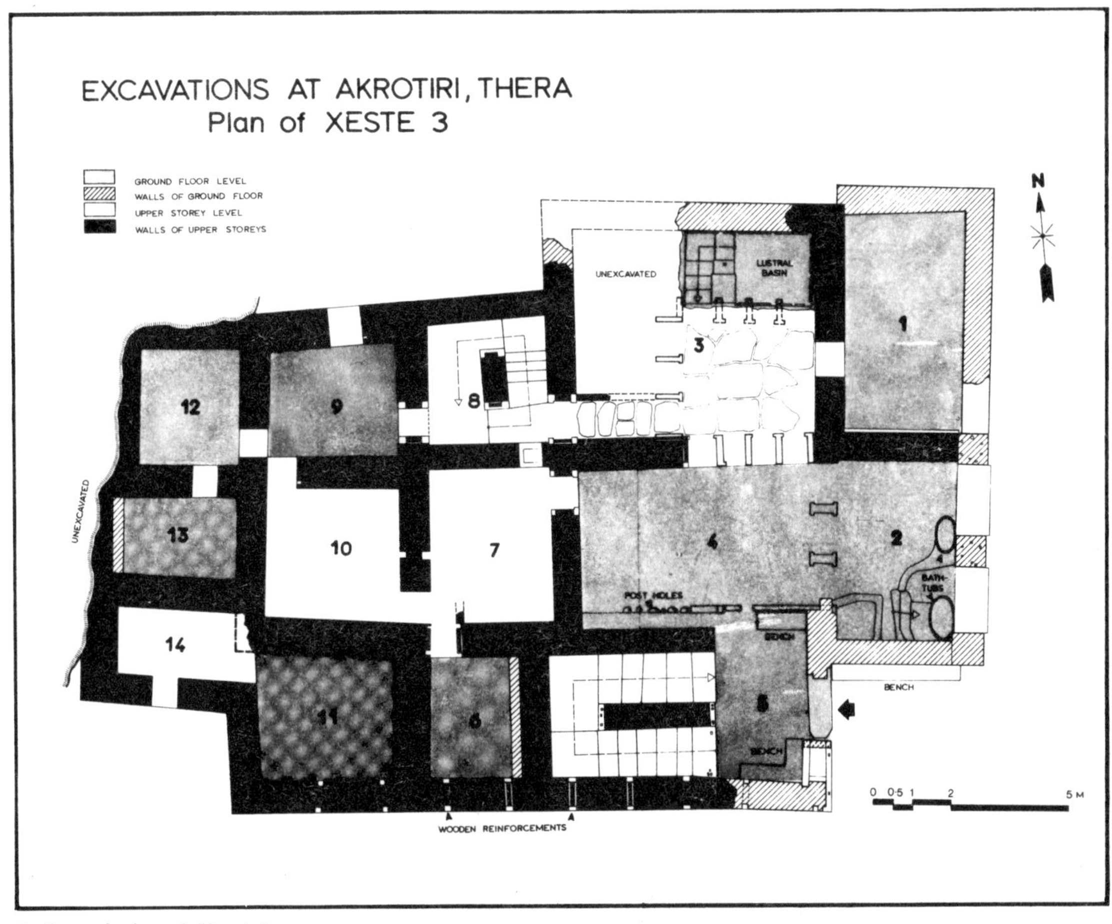

7 *Ground plan of Xesté 3.*

light entered the vestibule of each house even when the door was closed. It also permitted the person inside to check who was outside before opening the door. Another general rule seems to have been that basements should have small windows, probably to ensure standard conditions of temperature, humidity and ventilation since basement rooms were used for storing foodstuffs. Conversely, large windows were the norm in upper storeys where people lived and slept. Exceptions to this rule are rare and buildings with large windows at street level seem to have been shops or similar establishments. The large windows may have served as 'counters' or shop-windows, like the one opening onto Telchines Road from Room Delta 16, or onto the west side of Triangle Square from the House of the Anchor; the Pithoi Storeroom in Sector Alpha is another example.

plate 16

plate 13

Irregular, unworked stones and clay constituted the basic building materials at Akrotiri. In addition, timber reinforcements were used in the walls to strengthen them against earthquakes. The walls were encased in a series of horizontal frames built at intervals up the wall and connected by vertical timbers.

This method can be observed in buildings Xesté 2 and Xesté 3. Other ways of strengthening the walls were also employed. Successive sections might be set back from the street, thus creating corners which helped increase rigidity. Dressed stone blocks were used as cornerstones to consolidate these parts of the buildings still further. Similar ashlar masonry was used to frame doors and windows, to face special buildings (e.g. Xesté 4) and to form external friezes projecting slightly at each floor level in multi-storey houses.

plates 13, 14

Internal partition walls were built either of stone and clay mortar or of lighter materials, such as clay mixed with straw and reinforced with wooden beams, or large, thin sun-dried mud-bricks (in fact, mud-slabs), again prepared with the addition of chaff as a filler. Not surprisingly, the lighter materials were particularly common in the upper storeys.

Doors and windows were of wood. From marks scratched on the large stone thresholds, or impressions left in the volcanic ash, it seems that doors were either single or double. In both cases a shallow depression on the inner side of the threshold acted as the pivot hole. There must have been a corresponding hole, perhaps in the wooden frame (now perished), for the upper end of the pivot. Windows were probably protected with a transparent material–perhaps a kind of parchment–allowing light to enter yet preventing draughts and dust. Such a covering may not have been needed for the smaller windows since they had a wooden grille (the impressions of which can be observed in basement windows) which considerably reduced their aperture.

plates 19–21

Staircases were usually stone-built, though some were also of wood. No wooden staircases have survived, but there is proof of their existence from marks left on the adjacent walls. Very few of the stone staircases are completely solid, and even then, only in the lower treads. Beneath the majority there is a small room, the *sotto scala*. The substructure of each staircase consisted of a strong timber framework set between two parallel walls. A layer of earth and rubble was laid on top of this and then the actual stone steps. It is interesting to note that although the timberwork of the staircase was invariably supported by the adjacent walls, the stone treads were freely laid on the earth-rubble base. Thus it was easy to replace the treads when required, without interfering with the walls.

The floors at ground level and in basement rooms were of beaten earth, except in a few cases where ground-floor rooms were flagged or covered with broken sea-shells. The vestibule of a house was usually paved with slabs, as exemplified by the Mill House of Sector Alpha, the north entrance to Complex Delta, the vestibule of Xesté 3, and probably the House of the Ladies. In Room Alpha 2 of Sector Alpha (Pithoi Storeroom) the floor was of beaten earth mixed with crushed murex shells. The floors of the upper storeys were supported by wooden beams. Branches, reeds or rubble were laid on top of these beams and then covered with a layer of earth which often constituted the actual floor of the room. In special rooms, however, flagstones were arranged on top of the earth layer and the gaps between them often filled with painted plaster. In a very few cases broken murex shells were used for the floors of the upper storeys. Equally rare was a kind of primitive mosaic floor made of small sea pebbles mixed with a form of cement (as in rooms Delta 8 and Delta 18). The West House seems to have been roofed with a similar mosaic-like material, as fragments found in several places indicate. Otherwise the flat roofs appear to have been constructed along very similar lines to the upper floors.

It seems that the external walls of the buildings projected above the roof to form a kind of parapet around it. Rainwater was channelled away via long clay waterspouts onto the street below.

The outside and inner walls of the basements were covered with a coating of clay mixed with broken straw. Just occasionally the walls were coated with proper plaster, like the interiors of the upper storeys. This plaster varied in thickness from a few millimetres to a few centimetres and followed the uneven contours of the wall surface. It was smoothed while still wet, for which process sea pebbles were used–hundreds of them have been found in the excavation. These smoothed surfaces were then painted.

In large rooms the problem of roofing was solved by placing in the centre a circular stone base, on which stood a wooden pillar to support the beams of the ceiling–an arrangement also known from Crete. Central pillars, or rather their bases, have been found in both the ground floor and upper storey of Room 1 in Sector Alpha (Pithoi Storeroom), in the upper storey of Room 2 in Building Beta, in the 'shop' of Complex Delta (Delta 16) and elsewhere. One or two pillars of rubble and clay were sometimes used to support basement ceilings, as in the case of Room 1 in Complex Delta. When a room was so spacious that a pillar would have provided insufficient support for the ceiling, a pier-and-door partition *(polythyron)* was used. In the upper storey of Room Delta 1 one central line of doors was enough to unite the two sections of the hall. In both the ground and upper floors of Room 3 in Xesté 3 the *polythyra* formed three sides of a rectangle. A similar arrangement seems also to have existed on the third floor of the unexplored building, Xesté 4. This arrangement facilitated the creation of quite extensive halls, probably used for receptions or assemblies of people. The system of the *polythyron* also solved another problem; it ensured the intermediate illumination of internal rooms. Since houses were built as independent units, free on all sides, light-wells, common in the palatial architecture of Crete, are generally absent. Almost every room received direct light through a window. An exception to this norm seems to have been the House of the Ladies, where a very small internal room beside the staircase probably functioned as a light-well.

As a rule, ground-floor rooms and basements were used for storing goods and/or as workshops. Large jars *(pithoi)* were used as containers for various foodstuffs: several kinds of legumes, barley, flour, dried fruits, snails, dried fish and possibly wine and olive oil. Sometimes these jars were ranged along the wall, supported and separated by vertical stone or clay partitions. Sometimes they were partially buried in the ground, as in the case of the western half of

plates 22–24

Room Alpha 3 (Pithoi Storeroom), or were incorporated in built benches, as in the basement of Room Beta 1.

From the tools found in the basements it would seem that some kind of workshop was installed in each house, if only to serve the needs of its occupants. Stone hammers and anvils are very common finds.

In most of the houses discovered so far there is a mill installation. Its main feature is a heavy grinding stone affixed to a built bench, and a number of stone mortars, pestles and grinders comprise its necessary equipment. The mill installation is best exemplified by Room Delta 15, where there is also a jar incorporated into the same bench as the millstone, but at a lower level, to collect the flour. A very similar arrangement can be seen in the Mill House in Sector Alpha, where the flour seems to have been collected in portable containers placed in a niche beneath the small stone beams on which the millstone rested.

plate 25

There is no direct or convincing evidence that specific rooms were used as shrines or sanctuaries. However, the small room in the basement of Xesté 3, below the *polythyron* of Room 3, exhibits all the features of what is known, in the Cretan context, as a 'lustral basin'. It is accessible from above via a flight of steps and the lower parts of its walls were lined at intervals with rectangular stone slabs, the spaces between them evidently being filled with wood. Another room which may have had religious significance is Room Delta 2 (Room of the Lilies). Though bearing little or no resemblance to the 'lustral basin' of Xesté 3, it has certain characteristics which distinguish it from ordinary rooms. So far it is the only internal ground-floor room with wall-paintings. There is a door and a window on its eastern wall which look out onto an open space from which light is indirectly admitted. In the adjacent rooms to the east were found two plastered tripod 'offering tables' and two rhytons in the form of a boar's head. Moreover, in the same area, but outside the building, the only well-preserved pair of 'horns of consecration' was excavated. All these features suggest that this part of the site may have had a religious function.

It seems that the living quarters were restricted to the upper storeys of the houses. From the excavation data available so far, it is difficult to assign a specific function to each room (whether it was a bedroom, sitting room, reception hall or whatever). The only rooms which can be identified with certainty are the water closets. The best example of one has been found in the southwest corner of the upper storey of the West House as we have already noted. It consists of two built benches separated by a very narrow slit–about 10 cm wide–which are the seat and drain of the toilet respectively. At about floor level this drain consists of a cylindrical clay pipe. Just behind and above the toilet seat there is a niche in the wall, about 10 cm deep. Though most of the floor of the room has collapsed, it seems that originally it sloped towards the drainage hole. A bath tub, fragments of which were found among the ruins of the floor, seems to have stood to the left of the lavatory and a bronze tripod vessel found in association with this tub was probably none other then the Homeric *loetrochous,* with which water was poured into the bath. The 'bathroom' walls were coated with plaster

plates 17, 18

fig. 8

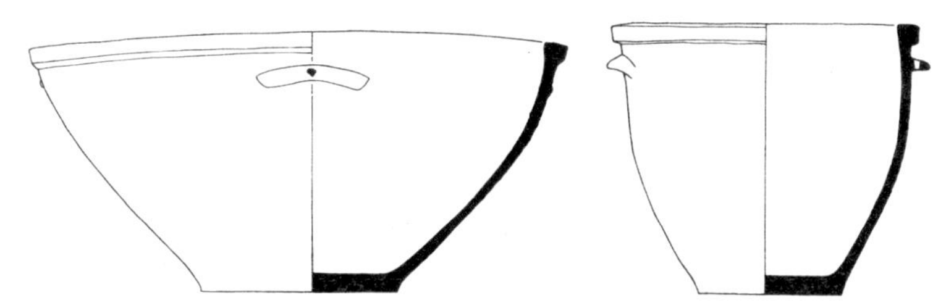

8 The bath tub found in Room 4 of the West House. Ht c. 60 cm.

painted a yellow ochre colour, though only halfway up their height, just that part likely to be splashed with water. This typical and well-preserved bathroom has proved an extremely useful source of information about similar installations both in Akrotiri and elsewhere. The Mill House of Sector Alpha also had a bathroom, probably separated from the rest of the room by a low partition wall. There is a similar shallow niche in the wall behind the toilet and its seat was probably wooden, as was apparently the case in the latrines of the Minoan palaces, where only the drainage holes are now visible. There is also evidence for lavatories in the House of the Ladies, in Building Beta and in Complex Delta at Akrotiri.

The Harbour

The city of Akrotiri must have been one of the most important ports in the Aegean during the Middle and Late Bronze Age. But, although the existence of a harbour can be assumed, it has not yet been excavated–indeed its location is still a matter for conjecture. From the present-day appearance of the coast it might seem unlikely that there could have been a harbour here, especially a sizeable one. However, careful observation of the area has indicated that the prehistoric coastline was quite different. Today's shore in fact consists of volcanic stones and tephra from the 'Minoan' eruption of the volcano. Before 1500 BC the sea must have been further inland, as has been shown by the well dug near the south gate of the site, where brackish water was struck at a depth of about 6 m in the layer of pumice and below the ash layer. When Mr Arvanitis, the owner of the land a few hundred metres to the west of the excavation, dug another well he struck salty water below the volcanic strata in a layer of fine sand, which very much resembled sand from the sea bed. If one can thus infer that the sea reached this point prior to the 'Minoan' eruption then this is of considerable importance, because the spot lies about 200 m inland, in the valley between the hill of Mesovouna (east) and the ridge of Mavro Rhachidhi (west). This location, sheltered by the surrounding hills, would have been ideal for the harbour of prehistoric Akrotiri. In my opinion, it is this harbour which is depicted in the wall-painting of the fleet from the West House. It is the harbour at the end of the voyage. The hilly landscape in the background is very reminiscent of the profile of the Mavro Rhachidhi ridge. The Late Bronze Age remains

fig. 2

on the crest of Mavro Rhachidhi lend weight to the argument, for they could be identified with the watchtower illustrated in the wall-painting.

Art

The Late Cycladic city of Akrotiri is, so far, unique in its wealth of wall-paintings. These are the ultimate artistic creations of Late Bronze Age society in the Aegean and reflect its aesthetic preferences.

The wall-painting technique is the same as that known from Crete. In this respect the role of Thera's large island neighbour was of paramount importance. For all upper-storey rooms, but rarely on the ground floor, a thin coat of lime plaster was applied on top of the normal wall surface of clay mixed with straw. In many cases the white plaster in its natural state was left as the background colour; when rubbed smooth, while still fresh, with sea pebbles, it often took on the appearance of polished ivory. Less often, yellow ochre or a pinkish pigment was applied over the whole of the plastered surface, the ochre being restricted mainly to the 'bathrooms'. Once the surface had been prepared guidelines were made in the wet plaster either with a taut string or a sharp instrument–perhaps an obsidian flake–thus outlining the figures or patterns to be painted. The technique was not true fresco except in a few instances, and these do not seem to have been deliberate. The artist probably began painting while the plaster was still wet, but made no effort to keep it wet as he continued, being content to complete the work on a dry surface. As a result, often in the same wall-painting, the paint has penetrated the plaster in some parts but flakes off easily elsewhere.

All the pigments used by the painters of Akrotiri seem to have been of mineral origin and have thus survived quite well. We do not know, however, what type of cohesive agent was used in preparing paints; presumably it was an organic glue that has left no trace, which would explain why the paintings have to be consolidated immediately they are discovered.

The repertoire of colours in the Theran wall-paintings includes white (the natural colour of the plaster), yellow, red, brown, blue and black. Besides being the usual background colour, white is also employed for exposed parts of the female body. Brown is the standard colour of the male body and, in addition, a secondary background shade, in landscapes, petals etc. Blue is used to depict water and, in some cases, perhaps as an alternative to grey (monkeys, shaved parts of the heads of juveniles), as well as for decorative motifs and details. Yellow is the standard colour for wooden structures, ornaments and, as we have already noted, the otherwise undecorated walls of bathrooms or latrines. Red is less common and usually delineates bands above and below pictures, although it is also characteristic of ornaments. Black may likewise be used for picture borders and as a secondary background colour, as well as for details and hair. These major colours also occur in intermediate shades which are, presumably, the result of mixing.

Thera and Akrotiri

1 The Thera volcano is still sporadically active, the focus of the eruptions being Nea Kameni, seen here from the town of Phira.

2 Modern Phira perches precariously on the edge of the caldera, above cliffs which fall sheer into the sea, 270 m below.

3 Airview from the east of the southern arc of Thera proper, showing the Akrotiri region centre left.

4 Excavations by R. Zahn near the present site in the early part of this century, with the modern village of Akrotiri in the background.

The excavations

5–7 Thick layers of volcanic debris had to be removed before the walls of the ancient houses began to emerge. A bulldozer was used to take off part of the topmost layer *(above)*. Excavations in 1969 revealed what became known as Building Gamma and Telchines Road (*left,* with Building Gamma on the right). A view inside Building Gamma *(below)* shows a door leading from one room to the next.

8 Part of the remarkable drainage system found underlying the northern section of Telchines Road.

9 A section through the layers of pumice which filled the space between the West House and the House of the Ladies.

10 A corrugated roof supported on Dexion pillars was erected over the whole site to protect the remains.

11 Conical-shaped cups fallen from an upper storey of Room 6 in the West House.

12 Pumice blocking the west propylon of Building Complex Delta (cf. plate 13).

Façades

13 Triangle Square, looking south, with Building Complex Delta on the left and the West House on the right. The west propylon (centre left) of Building Complex Delta shown in plate 12 has here been cleared of pumice.

14 The entrance to Room Delta 15, seen from the south.

15 The entrance to the West House. Here and in many places the buildings still stand two storeys high.

16 The southwest corner of the West House, viewed from Triangle Square (the struts are modern).

Water closets

17–18 The only rooms whose function can be identified with any certainty are the water closets. The best preserved one was found in the southwest corner of the upper storey of the West House. Consisting of two small benches divided by a narrow channel, it drained away into the sewers beneath the street via a cylindrical clay pipe. A bath tub may originally have stood to the left of the lavatory, together with a bronze tripod vessel with which water was poured into the bath.

Staircases

19–21 *(Above)* The entrance and staircase of Xesté 3, seen from the east. *(Right)* The collapsed staircase in the northern half of Building Delta. *(Below)* A side view of the West House staircase. The stone steps (shown here end-on near the top of the picture) rested on an earth base, which was itself supported by wooden beams (their holes are clearly visible).

Basement storerooms

22–24 Storage jars in the basements of Rooms Delta 1a *(left)*, Beta 1 *(above left)* and the Pithoi Storeroom of Sector Alpha *(above)*.

Mill installation

25 The mill installation in Room Delta 15.

The wall-paintings

26 The 'Boxing Children' and 'Antelopes' in Room Beta 1 (cf. plates IV and VIII).

27 One of the 'Ladies' from the house of that name, which probably decorated a corridor off Room 1. Facing east, she is clad in a characteristic Minoan-style dress.

28 Swallows dart among lilies on the walls of Room Delta 2. The rocky landscape – shown fully in plate III – covered the north, west and south sides of the room.

29 Part of the river landscape depicted on the upper frieze of the east wall of Room 5 in the West House. A panther-like creature pursues a pair of ducks among exotic trees and bushes beside a meandering river. (Cf. plate XV.)

30–32 Fragments from the group of the 'Saffron-gatherers', found in Room 3 (the 'lustral basin') of Xesté 3 and still in the process of restoration. Ladies are depicted offering a necklace *(above)*, seated on a rock *(below left)* and picking crocus stamens for saffron *(below right)*, a task which even today is performed exclusively by the womenfolk of Akrotiri.

Middle Cycladic and Helladic pottery

33 A Middle Cycladic potsherd with a representation of a human face, from Akrotiri.

34 A Middle Cycladic ewer from the graves in the Karageorghis Quarry.

35 A Middle Helladic cup from Akrotiri, imported from the Greek mainland.

36 A Middle Cycladic clay human figurine, from Akrotiri. Similar figurines made of marble have been found.

37 A Middle Cycladic clay figurine in the form of a bull, from Akrotiri.

38 A Middle Helladic jar found at Akrotiri, but imported from the Greek mainland.

The Theran artists were not daunted by problems of space for their compositions. They painted on large unbroken areas of wall, smaller areas interrupted by openings for doors and/or windows, narrow strips above and/or below a series of doors, windows or niches and even door and window jambs. All these surfaces were a challenge to the painter which he met in various ways, each time finding a new and original subject appropriate to the particular surface. The large walls of Room Beta 6 were covered with the magnificent composition of the 'Blue Monkeys' in a mountainous landscape. plate IX Similarly, the landscape with swallows and lilies was created for the walls of Room Delta 2. plate III Panels imitating the cabins of a ship embellished the walls of Room 4 of the West House. plate XI The composition with 'Ladies' was chosen for a special room in the house today named after them. plate VI The 'Ladies gathering Saffron' decorated the entire walls of the 'lustral basin' in Xesté 3. plates 30–32 In Room Beta 1 openings for doors and windows broke the surface of the walls and antelopes were cleverly juxtaposed to fit the space available, plate VIII pairs of them being depicted on the east and west walls, while another pair were made to face each other either side of a large window on the north wall. The narrower space between the southwest corner of the same room and a door leading into the adjacent room to the south was considered ideal for the 'Boxing Children'. plate IV Comparable surfaces in Room 5 of the West House on the north wall between its northeast corner and a window, and on the west wall between its southwest corner and a window, provided perfect panels for wall-paintings of a youth holding bunches of fish. plate XII The strips of wall above the windows and niches in Room 5 of the West House were covered with the frieze of the riverscape (east), flotilla (south) and sea-battle (north). plates XV, X, XIV The dado beneath the windows of the same room was painted in a marvellous imitation of polychrome marble. The surfaces above the *polythyra* in Xesté 3 also seem to have been covered with friezes: one shows blue monkeys performing human activities and another a running spiral motif. The window jambs in Room 4 of the West House were each covered by a wall-painting of a large pithos in which lilies were depicted. Finally, the so-called 'Young Priestess' holding an incense burner seems to have fallen from the jamb of the door connecting Rooms 4 and 5 in the West House. plate XIII

Framing seems to have been the dominant fashion in Theran art and architecture. Both the artist and the architect evidently felt the need to denote the limits of his work. Neither was content with the natural boundaries of the surface. The artist wanted his painting to be defined by its own boundaries and so be independent, in this respect, of the wall on which it was placed. This predilection is apparent in all the frescoes at Akrotiri. At the very least, the top and bottom of a picture are marked by a number of alternating coloured bands–borders at either side do not seem to have been quite so important and are usually missing. In this respect, perhaps, the painters were influenced by the ceramicists. On pottery the decoration is continuous except at the top and bottom of the vase.

From the number and size of wall-paintings found at Akrotiri, it may be assumed that several artists worked there during the Late Cycladic I period.

This inference is confirmed by a stylistic examination of the paintings–the hand of more than one artist can even be discerned in the same composition. It seems that there were 'schools' of artists, particularly on the evidence of a few paintings where errors of one hand have been corrected by another (pupil and master?). The artists must have had a high degree of freedom in the execution of their works, even if not in the choice of themes, which were perhaps selected or specified by those giving the commissions. As a result the paintings are remarkably unconventionalized, full of vitality and the breath of inspiration. This is in marked contrast to the frescoes of Crete, which adhere to the rigid conventions imposed by the ruling palaces. At Akrotiri art was not the monopoly of the monarch, as in the palaces of Crete, but was patronized by the more affluent members of a competitive society, who commissioned artists to paint their houses and enhance their surroundings, perhaps to impress their peers and rivals. Competition would have been encouraged among the artists, who each strove to create something innovative and original.

A whole range of subjects–both abstract or geometric and naturalistic or pictorial–comprise the iconography of the Theran wall-paintings. As a rule geometric motifs feature as complementary or secondary decorative elements in major compositions, e.g. the horizontal bands which delimit the upper and lower boundaries of the composition. In some cases solid brown rock-like motifs are suspended from the upper frame of alternating horizontal bands. In the wall-painting of the 'Ladies' these alternating coloured bands are wavy and describe arch-like curves above the female figures. The area of wall above these bands was filled with blue star motifs interconnected with red dots–perhaps in an attempt to illustrate the celestial arch. Among the geometric motifs used in the wall-paintings is the running spiral which occurs as a frieze above another subject, as in the case of the 'Blue Monkeys' from Room Beta 6, or independently, as in the case of friezes from Xesté 3.

plates VI, 27

plate IX

The rosette is another geometric motif which figures as a decorative element in the wall-paintings. It can be seen on the 'relief fresco' from Xesté 3, in which the rosettes fill the lozenge-shaped interstices described by the relief bands. A particularly impressive abstract design is the one imitating the marble dado in Rooms 4 and 5 of the West House.

plate V

Pictorial motifs used in the Akrotiri wall-paintings fall into four major categories: objects, floral, faunal and human. These motifs occur either in isolation or combined with landscapes. In the category of objects are included all man-made structures such as ships, buildings or towns. Isolated floral motifs are very rare and were, it seems, destined to cover surfaces of secondary importance. A stylized ivy branch ('sacral ivy') constitutes the frieze above the picture of the 'Boxing Children' and the 'Antelopes' of Room Beta 1. Lilies growing from jars were the subject chosen for the window jambs of Room 4 of the West House, while one wall of a room in the House of the Ladies was covered with papyrus plants.

plate 26

The wall-paintings in which animals and humans are depicted may all be described as 'narrative'. The term may even be applied when these figures appear in isolation, as in the case of the 'Antelopes' from Room Beta 1: though not shown in a specific setting, they display a narrative element in that one of the antelopes turns its head full of expression back to face the one following. The 'Fishermen' from Room 5 of the West House, although static, have 'something to say' in the proud manner in which they display their catch. This tendency holds also for the 'Young Priestess' from the same room, who is performing some 'ritual' act, as well as for the scene of women from the House of the Ladies which, despite its damaged state, may be described as 'narrative' because of the attitudes of the figures and their gestures. More explicitly 'narrative' is the scene of the 'Boxing Children' from Room Beta 1. Both figures wear a boxing glove on one hand and, while one child aims to strike a blow, the other, using his raised arm as a shield, prepares to attack with his gloved hand.

plate VIII
plate XII
plate XIII
plate VI
plates IV, 26

This preference for narrative scenes is more apparent in the landscapes with animals. The mountainous landscape in the painting of the 'Lilies' (Room Delta 2) has been interpreted as depicting the mating time of the swallows which dart and fly joyfully among the blossoming lilies. The so-called 'Nilotic' landscape of the east frieze from Room 5 of the West House reveals a great deal about the wild life of this riparian environment, with its mixture of real and imaginary creatures. A griffin flies over the river, a wild cat stalks some ducks, one of which flies away in fear over clusters of palm trees bent by violent winds. The scenes in the 'miniature frescoes' from the same building, in which human figures are involved, surpass all the other paintings in their narrative impact since they are truly action-packed. The 'Flotilla' tells the story of a voyage from one harbour to another. Whatever the historical or other significance of this event, the artist has successfully 'told the story': a fleet of ships sets sail from a harbour town, the inhabitants of which come to the water's edge to bid it farewell. The voyage seems to be a joyful undertaking, as the presence of dolphins leaping above the water indicates. At its destination, another harbour town, the flotilla receives a friendly welcome from the townsfolk who have gathered at the quayside or on the roofs of their houses, or have already gone out in a small rowing boat to meet the first vessel. Meanwhile, the wild creatures shown in the background continue their perennial struggle for survival. Deer try desperately to escape from a pursuing lion.

plates III, 28
plates XV, 29
plate X

More action is shown in the other 'miniature fresco' from the north wall of Room 5 of the West House. Here the artist has managed to convey various aspects of life by superimposing unrelated scenes. These seem to be happening simultaneously in the same area: their superimposition is perhaps an artistic device to denote dimension. The scene in the foreground takes place at sea, not far from the shore, and depicts a shipwreck. The human bodies lying on the bottom in odd positions may be the drowned victims. Next in series, lower middle distance, there is a group of warriors, armed in the Mycenaean manner, marching along the quayside. On the next plane, young women return from a well with their water-filled pitchers balanced on their heads; young men flirt

plate XIV

with them. Very near the well is a pen into which two shepherds drive their flocks of sheep and goat.

plates 30–32

Yet another group of wall-paintings, still undergoing restoration, is clearly narrative in content. In a mountainous landscape, beautifully attired young women are shown picking stamens from the saffron crocus. The stamens are collected in small baskets which are then emptied into a larger one placed in front of a majestic female figure flanked by a griffin and a blue monkey. A young girl is shown seated on a rock, suffering from a wounded toe, as is expressed by the way in which she supports her forehead with the left hand, whilst holding the sore foot with her right hand. This magnificent composition comes from the building known as Xesté 3. From the same area we now have another important wall-painting, again still being restored. This is a frieze showing blue monkeys performing human activities: one is brandishing a sword, another seems to be playing a harp or lyre.

The good state of preservation of the ruins at Akrotiri and the sophisticated techniques used in recovering and restoring the wall-paintings have meant that, for the first time, the finest examples of this magnificent art of the prehistoric Aegean can be seen in all their glory. This is perhaps the main reason why international interest has focussed on the site. As a response to this several attempts have been made by scholars to interpret the paintings. No theory can succeed, however, without taking into consideration the social context. So far all the paintings have come from private houses, not public buildings. Surely, therefore, they were primarily of personal importance. The householder will have taken pride in his own frescoes since they reflected his economic and social status. They may indeed have depicted those activities which secured his position in the social and economic hierarchy.

fig. 10

The location of the paintings inside the house may also have been significant and thus have a bearing on their interpretation. For example, the 'Room of the Lilies' (Delta 2) in Building Complex Delta is the only ground-floor room, discovered so far, to be decorated with wall-paintings. The adjacent rooms to the east have produced objects which are usually considered to be for ritual use (tripod offering tables, rhytons in the form of a boar's head etc.). The only complete pair of 'horns of consecration' was also found outside the east wall of this building. One could argue therefore that Room Delta 2 had some cult significance and also, by implication, the wall-painting entitled 'The Coming of Spring'. A similar chain of reasoning may be applied to the large composition of

fig. 7

the 'Ladies gathering Saffron', which apparently embellished the walls of the 'lustral basin' in Xesté 3. Since this area is, in Minoan archaeology, conventionally considered sacred, the scene in the wall-painting may be interpreted as having religious significance. Indeed, the central female figure who appears to be supervising the operation is flanked by an exotic animal (monkey) and a mythical one (griffin), and may be a deity to whom the saffron stamens are offered. On the other hand, the owner of Xesté 3 could have been a merchant involved in the collection and/or distribution of saffron, in which case the paintings may depict mundane activities (albeit in a rather stylized way for artistic effect).

Elsewhere it is even harder to argue for a religious interpretation of the paintings. For example, the frescoes from the west wing of the upper storey of the West House have themes connected with the sea (fishermen, flotilla, sea-battle) or with ships (cabins in Room 4). Here it is clear that the aim of the painter was to express the status of his patron and Marinatos, quite rightly, recognized that the owner of this house was the admiral of the flotilla of the 'miniature fresco'. However one interprets the Theran wall-paintings, all scholars will agree that they constitute a precious source of information about life at Akrotiri in Minoan times–about people's activities, their knowledge of the world outside, and the natural and manmade environment. Hairstyles, fashion in dress, jewelry and everyday pursuits are revealed in rich detail. The 'Flotilla' fresco provides information about Aegean ships and sailing techniques never before encountered on such a scale. And many paintings give vital clues about the flora and fauna of the ancient Aegean (it is intriguing that some landscapes are very reminiscent of Thera today, for instance the 'Monkey' painting, or 'the Coming of Spring').

figs 5, 10

The artists drew their subjects with such conviction that one can only assume they were working from first-hand experience. For the more exotic landscapes they must either have visited foreign parts personally or heard extraordinarily vivid descriptions from others. How else could they have painted the lifelike deer, antelopes, wild cats or lions we see in the frescoes? None of these animals were indigenous to the Aegean. Of the non-Aegean species in the paintings, only the blue monkey might have been present on Thera, imported from Egypt as a pet or performing animal.

Description of individual wall-paintings

Sector Alpha

In a small room named the 'Porter's Lodge' by Marinatos, adjacent to the South Corridor of Sector Alpha, fragments of wall-paintings were found which had fallen from the upper storey. The whole area had been badly eroded by seasonal floods along the modern ravine, and the frescoes were in poor condition. As yet this part of the site has not been completely excavated, so the exact nature of the whole painting is unclear. Judging from the individual fragments, it must have been quite an important composition. One group of fragments shows a man (Marinatos called him the 'African') in front of a bent palm tree. Another group shows blue monkeys apparently surrounding a structure surmounted by 'horns of consecration' and supported by columns terminating in papyrus flowers(?). Finally, a third group of fragments shows flying birds. All these fragments seem to be closely associated, but it is impossible to reconstruct the whole composition from them.

fig. 5

Building Beta

fig. 9 This building, too, has only been partially excavated, and the excavated sector has suffered from erosion along the modern ravine. Two rooms (Beta 6 and Beta 1) have produced important wall-paintings. The southeast half of Room Beta 6 had been badly damaged by seasonal flooding, but sufficient fresco fragments were recovered for a rocky landscape with eight blue monkeys clambering over it to be reconstructed. (plate IX) The lower limit of the composition is defined by wide wavy bands, the upper part by a frieze of spirals between two groups of horizontal bands. It seems that the design spread over at least two walls of Beta 6. Unfortunately the damaged condition of a number of fragments, showing flying swallows as well as parts of other animals (a goat?), makes it extremely difficult to suggest their position within the room. It is possible that the fragments with the 'goat' belonged to an earlier wall-painting, fragments of which were embedded within the thick plaster when the room was redecorated.

The situation in Room Beta 1 is much clearer. This is not because the fragments are better preserved–in fact many are in a more fragile condition–but because more of them were recovered. The excavators, having acquired experience in the previous season, also applied more systematic methods of removing and recording the position of the fragments. The upper storey of Beta 1 was divided into two by a partition wall of sun-dried bricks running from north to south. The wall surface in the eastern part of the room was interrupted by five openings: three on the south wall, one on the east and one on the west. A niche flanked by two doors on the south wall left only a narrow panel at the southwest corner. (plates IV, 26) This was decorated with the magnificent wall-painting of the 'Boxing Children'. Marinatos originally suggested that these might be 'two princely brothers', but later, in accordance with his predisposition to see a religious significance in all the paintings, he referred to them as 'divine beings'. He came to this conclusion because of their blue heads, which he connected with epithets describing the hair of gods and heroes in the Homeric poems (e.g. blue-maned Poseidon, blue-eyebrowed Zeus, and Hera, blue-bearded Odysseus). However, on inspecting the human figures in the Theran wall-paintings as a whole, it has been noted that the use of blue in depicting the hair is always associated with young persons, judging from their features (e.g. 'Boxing Children', two 'Fishermen' from the West House, the so-called 'Young Priestess', some of the female 'Saffron-gatherers'). I therefore venture to suggest that blue on the head denotes youth: perhaps the heads of young people were partially shaved or cut and a few rich curly locks allowed to grow, or perhaps they wore some kind of head-cover through which the ringlets fell. The mural of the 'Boxing Children' may simply illustrate a game between two youths.

The west, north and east walls of Room Beta 1 were covered with paintings of six antelopes. The continuity of planes was interrupted by the large window on the north wall. (plates VIII, 26) A single antelope was shown on either side of this window and a pair of them on the east and west walls. The pair on the west wall was the best preserved of all. The bodies of the animals were outlined in a clear black

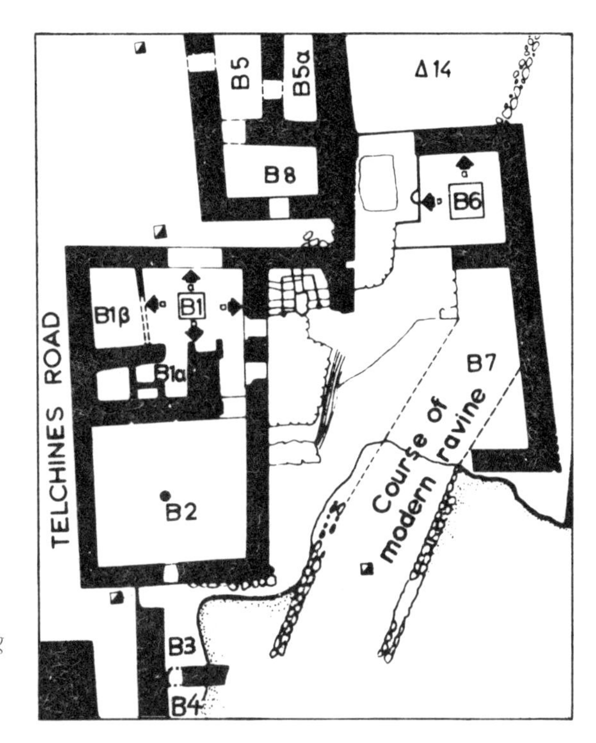

9 Plan of Building Beta, showing the location of the frescoes (arrowed). See also fig. 5.

line, while the heads were drawn in greater detail, some features shown in red. To quote Marinatos, 'the animation and vitality achieved is indeed astounding. The pair depicted here are in amorous converse, as is shown by the movement of their heads, lips and tails.'

The whole of Room Beta 1 was crowned by a frieze of stylized ivy with blue leaves growing from a red stalk.

Building Gamma

Fragments of wall-paintings were found in the area of Room Gamma 10 as well as the adjacent open space ('Northern Court'). Although this sector has not been systematically excavated yet, the fragments are big enough for us to have some idea of the subject of the paintings. Rosettes are scattered at random on a plain white ground and at either side of a group of wavy bands. Marinatos interpreted the rosettes as being imitations of a kind of clay mail, used in Sumer as an architectural decorative element: there they were affixed to the walls so as to form a kind of mosaic over the wall surface. *fig. 5*

Complex Delta

Only one room in this large building unit has wall-paintings (Delta 2), and it is the only room, so far, in which the paintings have been found in situ. The north, west and south walls were covered with a painting of the same theme, the fourth wall, the east, was interrupted by a door, a window and a niche. *fig. 10*

Depicted on the three walls is a rather mountainous landscape with multi-coloured rocks (red, light-blue, yellow and dark green). The colour and morpho- plates III, 28

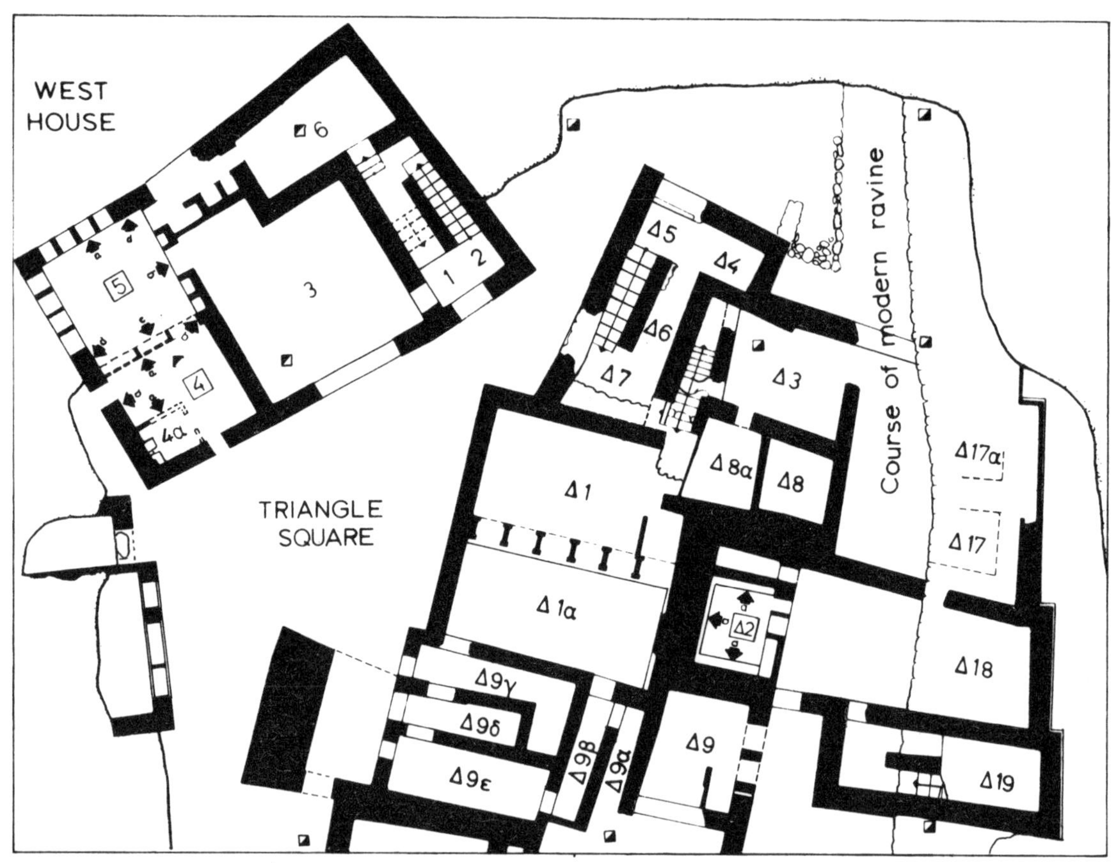

10 Plan of the West House and Building Complex Delta, showing the location of the frescoes (arrowed). See also figs 5 and 6.

logy of the rocks is such that the artist may have wished to show a Theran landscape and, indeed, Marinatos went so far as to declare that 'this wall-painting represents an unhoped opportunity for geologists in that it gives a glimpse of Thera before the eruption'. Clusters of blooming lilies grow from the rocks, their yellow leaves and stems projected against the white background. The lilies are shown on a much larger scale than the rocks, and between or above them swallows fly either singly or in pairs. It is here that the artist's audacity is most manifest. The birds are shown in very naturalistic poses, betraying the artist's keen observation of–and familiarity with–their habits. The pairs of birds on the west and north walls in particular led Marinatos to speak of 'amorous twittering swallows'. He also noted the artist's preference for triads: three rocks are depicted on each of the three walls and, except for two instances on the west and south walls, there are three lily stems growing from each rock. Perhaps it was this repetition of triads which led Marinatos to interpret the whole composition as 'a religious conception of the great Spring festival under the patronage of the Spring goddess of Nature... It wants to express the advanced Spring season when the swallows, who have come back, are restless from mating fever and are feverishly preparing their nests.' Evidence which may corroborate the religious interpretation of this part of Complex Delta has already been presented (p. 76).

It is interesting to note that nowadays swallows do not nest on Thera. Marinatos' somewhat romantic idea that 'the eruption was so terrifying as to uproot even the migrating instinct' is hardly sufficient explanation. The swallows' absence may rather be attributed to the uncohesiveness of the island's soil today, which is of volcanic ash, and the lack of clay for nest-building. Swallows do not breed either on Stromboli, an Aeolian island off the coast of Italy which is also covered with volcanic ash.

The House of the Ladies

Excavations here are still far from complete. The house was named after the wall-paintings found in it depicting female figures dressed in Minoan garments. Much of the building (the area following the west-east slope of the overlying field) has been badly damaged by erosion. In the middle of the North Wing an oblong room (Room 1) was decorated with wall-paintings in its upper storey, although the paintings are poorly preserved. A transverse north-south wall divided Room 1 into two parts and the floor in both parts of the third storey was paved with large flags. On the walls of the western sector of the room there were murals illustrating clusters of rather large plants in blossom. Marinatos identified the plants as sea daffodils *(Pancratium maritimum)*, but in order to do so he had to suppose that they were painted in an 'extraordinary size', something which is unusual in Minoan art. Another interpretation, proposed by Peter Warren, that the flowers depicted are clusters of papyrus, seems altogether more likely. Although much of the wall-painting has been lost, enough has sur-

fig. 11

plate VII

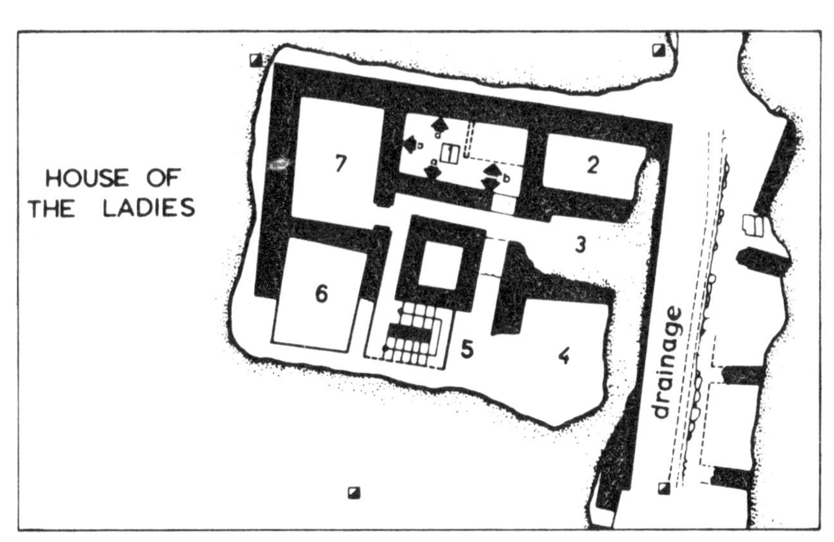

11 Plan of the House of the Ladies, showing the location of the frescoes (arrowed). See also fig. 5.

vived for us to be able to comprehend the composition as a whole. From small hillocks grow clusters of papyrus plants, silhouetted against the white background of the wall. Above the plants alternating bands of blue, white and red form a rather wide frieze which probably ran round the entire room.

The door connecting the two halves of Room 1 seems to have been at the southern end of the partition wall, as is demonstrated by the unpainted white plaster on the south wall, between the murals in the western and eastern parts of the room. The width of this unpainted surface seems to correspond to the thickness of the transverse wall. Another wall, made of mud-bricks or clay, probably partitioned off the northeast corner of Room 1, and there is strong evidence to suggest that this corner was arranged as a bathroom.

Between this partition wall and the solid south wall of the room a passage was formed which led to the Room of the Papyruses. The famous frescoes of the 'Ladies' probably decorated the walls of this corridor. On the south wall stood a lady, clad in the characteristic Minoan-style dress and facing east; unfortunately, the eastern part of the composition is missing. On the north wall another lady, similarly attired but with bared breasts, also faced east, leaning with outstretched arms towards another female figure, probably seated, of which only part of the dress has survived. Thus it seems that the murals on both walls belonged to a unified composition: a kind of procession of women advancing towards some person or object, now lost, on the east wall. The women on both walls are shown under a series of three alternating wavy bands of black and blue. The whole of the wall above these bands was covered with blue stars interspersed with red dots.

plates VI, 27

As for the interpretation of the frescoes in Room 1, Marinatos attributed religious significance to the plant mural, identifying the flowers with the *Pancratium* lily in order to support his view that 'the probability is great that the supernatural sea daffodils have a special religious meaning'. We have already noted, however, that the flowers are more likely to be papyruses, and there is no archaeological evidence to substantiate the religious theory. Nevertheless it is quite probable that the ladies from the same room belonged to a religious scene. Their clothes, their arrangement in a kind of procession in an easterly direction and the bending of their bodies all favour such an interpretation. Another reason why Marinatos insisted that the room was of a religious character was the discovery of a number of built clay chests or cists which contained different vases. However, these chests were found under the paved floor of the third storey and there is no evidence of there being direct communication between the second and the third storeys. The chests cannot therefore necessarily be considered to have served as 'sacral repositories which confirm beyond any doubt the sacral character of the room'.

West House

figs 6, 10

At the time of its discovery this building was at the westernmost edge of the excavated area, hence its name, the West House. At one time it possessed two (at the west) and possibly three (at the northeast) storeys. The upper storey of the west wing was divided by thin partition walls into three rooms. Room 4a occupies the southwest corner of the building and accommodated the lavatory and bathroom. Immediately to the north of Room 4a was a long narrow space (Room 4) and beyond it a large room (Room 5) in the northwest corner of the building. Both Room 4 and Room 5 were embellished with magnificent murals.

Room 4 This room is L-shaped in plan and its reconstruction in Marinatos, *Thera VI, (Plates),* Drawing 4 is quite arbitrary. The L-shaped plan is due to the arrangement of the bathroom at the southwest corner of the building. Painted on the jambs either side of the window in the west wall are large jars from which spring five lilies in full bloom. Of particular interest is the artist's attempt faithfully to record the material from which these vases were made: polychrome veined marble. The window sill and the lower parts of the window jambs, on which the vases were standing, were similarly painted.

The walls of Room 4 were decorated with a single motif which was repeated eight times. Marinatos originally christened this theme a 'banner', but later identified it as the 'cabin' at the stern of the ships depicted in the so-called miniature fresco (see below). The motifs look like screens betwen three upright poles each topped by an Egyptian lily. The space below the lilies is divided into three horizontal zones by three straight and one wavy band, the ends of which project laterally beyond the vertical poles. This would suggest that they represent actual structural members, possibly beams maintaining the poles. The decoration on these bands or beams–different in each screen–consists of spirals, crosses, locks etc. Festoons or garlands of flowers or rosettes–each being different–hang from the poles between the top horizontal band and the second wavy one. The uppermost limit of each screen is demarcated by a wavy band. The panels of the screen were of ox-hide, rendered by patches differently on each one. All the screens are depicted above a continuous dado painted in imitation of veined polychrome marble, which apparently ran round the whole of the room. The fact that these 'cabins' are shown completely free and independent on the walls, as well as their sophisticated embellishment, suggests that they may illustrate palanquins or litters, the covers of which may be represented by the top horizontal band. Marinatos sought a religious significance in his interpretation of these motifs as 'banners' or 'cabins'. He said of the 'banner': 'it is probable that we must understand it to be a religious implement serving in some manner to the fertility rites.' He also stated that the 'repetition of the cabin eight times' and 'the presence of the priestess' (see below) suggests that there must have been a special ceremony for the 'dynasty of the captains' of the West House comparable with the 'offering of incense by the Pharaoh in the Room of the Ancestors'. However, the idea of palanquins cannot be rejected since such devices were not lacking from Minoan society, as the archaeological evidence suggests.

plate XI

The 'Young Priestess' In the northeast corner of Room 4, 'as by a miracle, an intact figure of a young priestess, over 1 m high' was discovered. With these

plate XIII

words Marinatos first announced the finding of this work of art. In his reconstruction plan of the upper storey he placed the painting on the north wall of Room 4, next to a group of 'screens'. However, its height 'over 1 m' does not correspond with that of the 'screens', which are 1.83 m high. In fact the dimensions of the 'priestess' painting are closely related to those of a jamb of the door connecting Rooms 4 and 5. If one considers the position in which the fresco was found, it would seem that it originally adorned one of the jambs (probably the west one) of the door. Marinatos identified the female as a 'young priestess' because of her long heavy garment and the fact that she 'holds with her right hand a metal vase, to be understood as made of gold and silver, fluted and bearing a long, straight handle'. Although he admitted that a class of pottery braziers are 'akin to vases', he stated that 'no real parallel of such a vase of metal or clay' exists. In fact, since the discovery of this painting, a similar bronze brazier has been found, though poorly preserved. The existence of a large number of clay braziers of the same type leaves us in no doubt as to what the 'young priestess' is holding: a metal brazier or incense burner full of glowing charcoal, shown in dark red. The 'young priestess' is sprinkling something–perhaps incense–over the brazier with her right hand. Marinatos' argument against the interpretation of the vase as a brazier, on the grounds that 'as the girl holds the vase by the bottom instead of by the handle, and as a metal vase is meant, it is impossible to explain the red matter inside the vase as charcoal', is not particularly strong since a layer of ash would have been arranged under the charcoal, to keep it burning for longer and to prevent the heat from affecting the brazier. Otherwise even the handle would have been too hot to grasp. There is no actual evidence to support his interpretation of the red matter as being 'a kind of cake' or a 'fig pudding'. The young lady shown on the door jamb, whether a priestess or girl of the household, seems to be moving from Room 4 to Room 5 or vice versa, censing the house with some aromatic substance. Whether this was done for any religious purpose or merely to purify the air–there is a lavatory installation adjacent–is difficult to decide. Perhaps for both reasons.

plate 44

fig. 12

Room 5 Each of the outer walls of this room (on the north and west) had four windows. The east wall likewise had two doors and three niches, and similar niches may once have punctuated the south wall. Because of all these openings the surfaces available for painting were restricted: narrow friezes above and below the windows, and two panels, one on the north wall at its easternmost extremity and one on the west wall at its southern end. Both these panels were decorated with paintings of a naked youth holding bunches of fish. The 'Fisherman' of the northeast corner is the best preserved of the two and, apart from being detached from the wall, was found intact. This led Marinatos to propose that it was a portable painting, but his supporting arguments have not been substantiated by excavation. The painting exactly fits the space available at the east end of the north wall. In particular, the height of the fresco–identical to that of the nearby windows–exactly covers the area between the two friezes, above and below the windows. Marinatos also suggested that the youth was circumcised,

plate XII

but again without foundation. He was, however, correct in stating that 'it is the first time that the classical nudity appears on a mortal male of the Minoan period, with the exception of small children'. The refined profile of the face, the outline of the body, the naturalism and perspective with which the fish are rendered–these are all features rarely found in prehistoric Aegean art. The youth, his head partially shaved, proudly holds a bunch of fish in each hand.

Equally splendid is the young 'Fisherman' from the southwest corner of Room 5. He is depicted entirely in profile and with both hands holds a bunch of fish. Unfortunately this wall-painting is badly damaged.

Room 5 (lower frieze) Beneath the windows of the north and west walls of Room 5 ran a frieze or dado painted in imitation of polychrome marble. It is characteristic that this theme was repeated in both Rooms 4 and 5 of the West House, in the latter extending beyond the windows and under the panel with the Fishermen.

The dado was divided into panels, as in Room 4, by broad vertical yellow bands, as if each panel represented a polychrome marble plaque. The bands corresponded in width and position to the wooden partitions between the windows and were obviously meant to be painted imitations of them. Rising from floor level they created the illusion that they supported the window-sills, thus giving an impression of strength to the structure.

Room 5 (upper friezes) Above the windows and niches Room 5 was apparently decorated with friezes, each one with a different theme. There is still some doubt as to whether the west wall had such a frieze, since no evidence for one has yet come to light. Perhaps the artist(s) had not finished their work when the volcano erupted in 1500 BC (the walls of the southeast corner of Room 4, opposite the bathroom, may also never have been completed).

The upper friezes of the north, east and south walls, as they have been reassembled and located from the myriad fragments, were as follows:

Room 5 (upper frieze: north wall) Because of the mutilated and fragmentary condition of this frieze the theme is difficult to understand. Two groups of fragments have been reassembled, each showing a different subject, though they both seem to be integral parts of a general story narrated along the north wall. One of these groups, poorly preserved, shows a gathering of men on a hill. The men are dressed in different garments and some of them are youths with Minoan loincloths. They all advance towards a central scene on top of the hill. The meaning of this picture is difficult to comprehend; Marinatos spoke about 'tension of their spirits and a moment of crisis'. Iakovides, on the other hand, interprets the scene as a gathering at a mountain sanctuary.

The other group of fragments is better preserved. Three different scenes are depicted on three different levels, an attempt by the artist to give his painting perspective. In the foreground, partly preserved, lie several ships near a rocky seashore. On one of them stands a man at the prow holding a long spear upright. The prow of the ship below seems to have been broken. Only the stem of a third ship, on the right, has been preserved. Between these three vessels,

plate XIV

12 A conjectural reconstruction of Room 5 in the West House, looking east. From left to right, the frescoes on the walls are: the 'Sea Battle', the 'Fisherman', the 'River Landscape' and the 'Flotilla'. See also figs 20 and 21.

three men are shown in unnatural positions. Three rectangular objects lying near the men are easily recognizable as ox-hide shields. A hooked instrument next to the third man was probably for grappling ships. The odd position of the men is probably an attempt by the artist to portray drowned warriors. Whether they were victims of a sea-battle or shipwreck is a matter for conjecture. The vessels seem definitely to have been warships, however, or at least they carried warriors. A building was depicted on the rocks in front of the shipwreck, but only its left edge has been preserved.

Immediately above the scene of the shipwreck, at the water's edge, is a single-storey building with four openings, two of which are painted greyish-black and two left the natural white of the plaster. One of the white openings is well pre-

served and frames a man clad in a dark garment, who faces right and carries a long stick on his shoulder. From vestiges preserved in the other white opening it can be surmised that here too was a similar picture, except that the person was dressed in a white garment with a red border. On the same plane, to the right of the building, is a detachment of warriors, marching in single file to the right. Five warriors are well preserved, but there were surely more. They wear leather helmets to which boar's tusks are affixed, which Marinatos aptly named the Amyntorian helmet. This is the earliest type of Mycenaean helmet which, according to tradition, Amyntor kept in his home at Eleon in Phokis. From there it was stolen by Autolykos who offered it to Amphidamos of Kythera who, in turn, gave it as a present to his Cretan guest Molus. Molus passed it on to his son Meriones who participated in the Trojan War, which is why this type of helmet is also known to archaeologists as Meriones' helmet. The warriors also carry a long spear in the right hand and long rectangular ox-hide shields hung from around the neck. These shields conceal the soldiers' bodies entirely and only the lower part of the sword sheath with its terminal tassle projects to one side. Whether the warriors are invaders or merely landing in a friendly place after an arduous voyage is, again, a matter for conjecture. There are no other indications in the picture that the soldiers are hostile, but Marinatos spoke of this scene as being an attack, launched to disrupt the peaceful life of the mountain. For the scene in the background does, indeed, show the peaceful countryside. Two shepherds are driving their flock into a circular enclosure, evidently to pen them in the shade of the two trees whose trunks form the gate of the fold. In front of the pen a spring or well is shown as a small structure with water jars placed on top. Two women move away from the spring, to the right, their pitchers balanced confidently on their heads. A group of men–four are preserved–dressed in clothes of assorted hues, seemingly watch something going on in the opposite direction. As has been mentioned earlier, the scene is that of a familiar Aegean environment with the spring as its focal point, since water is a precious commodity, especially during the summer months. The flock is being driven to the spring, to be watered, and then to the pen to rest. The women come to the spring for water for their households. And, finally, at the spring the men congregate, not only to 'freshen their lips' but to watch and flirt with the girls of their village, away from prying eyes.

Marinatos interpreted this scene as an invasion of Mycenaean warriors from the sea against a peaceful village in Libya. He recognized North African sheep among the animals shown in the uppermost level of the painting. In order to support his Libyan theory he declared that the bodies lying in the water were Libyans too. One of them, according to Marinatos, was carrying a shield made of ostrich feathers. Even though this body is only 5–6 cm in size, Marinatos recognized a man circumcised in the Libyan fashion, and so endorsed his theory. But neither the landscape nor these aforementioned details are sufficiently convincing evidence.

There are several other interpretations of the miniature fresco based on Marinatos' Libyan theory. According to S. Stucchi the friezes of all three walls–north, east and south–relate successive events in the same story, beginning with the north wall: A Minoan colony in Libya is attacked by Libyans from inland; the Minoan ships come to their rescue; the bodies in the water belong to Libyans who have fallen in the struggle; the warriors are the defenders of the colony and are shown pursuing the Libyan attackers, who must have been drawn in the missing part of the mural. According to Stucchi, the figures shown above the houses are children who, copying the men, play at war. The enclosure is not a pen but a Minoan temenos, 'with two sacred trees, probably olive trees'.

The idea of a battle is also favoured by M. Benzi who, however, does not place it in North Africa, but within the Aegean. He considers the ships in the

Late Cycladic pottery from Akrotiri

39 A clay rhyton in the form of a triton shell.

40 A clay rhyton in the form of a lion's head.

41 A clay rhyton in the form of a bull.

42 An ostrich egg made into a rhyton.

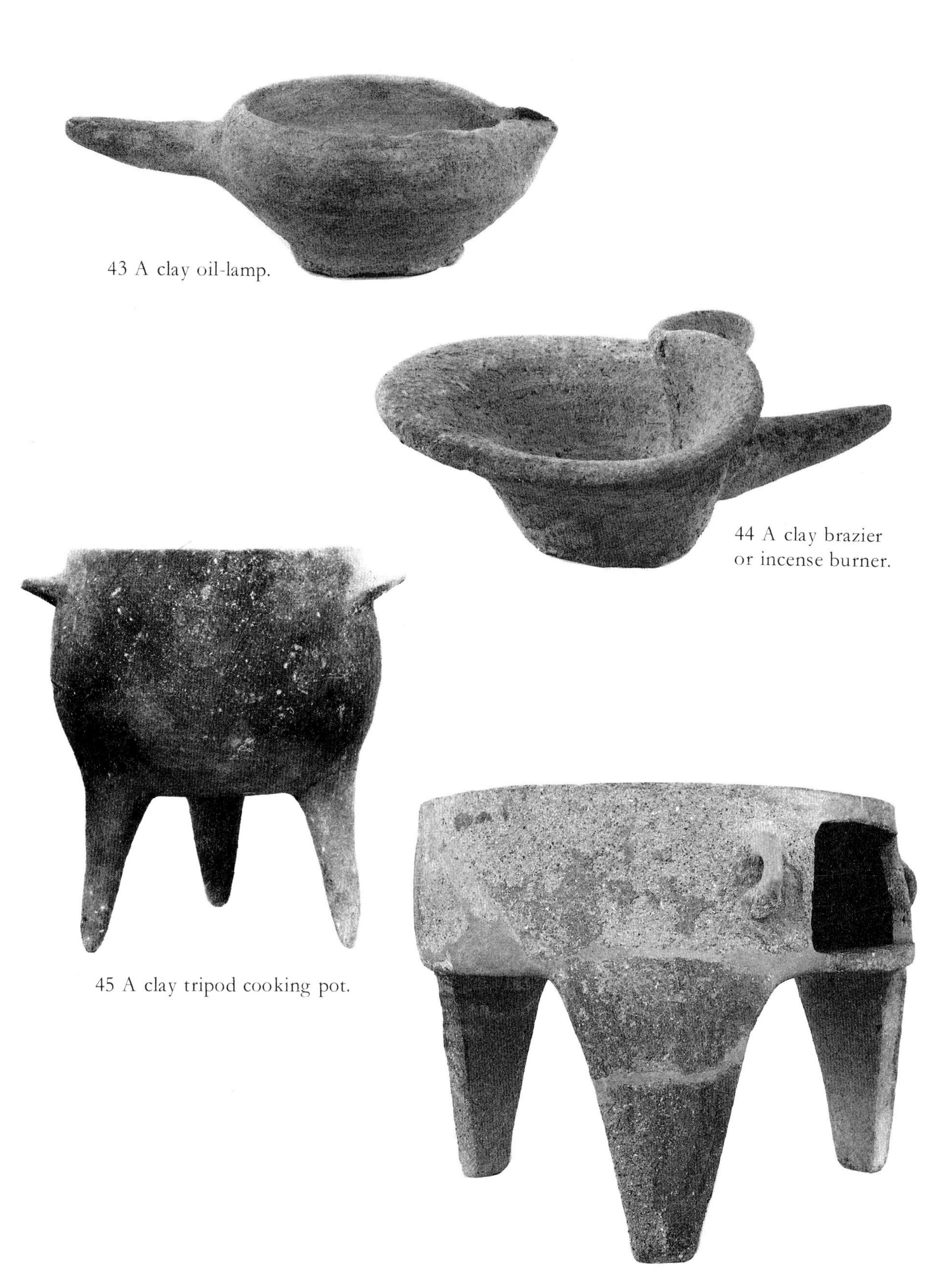

43 A clay oil-lamp.

44 A clay brazier or incense burner.

45 A clay tripod cooking pot.

46 A portable clay tripod 'cooker'.

47 A local bridge-spouted pithos with painted linear decoration.

48 An imported ewer with painted linear decoration.

49 A local bridge-spouted ewer with dark-on-light floral motifs.

50 A local beak-spouted ewer with dark-on-light floral motifs.

51 A local ewer with dark-on-light floral motifs.

52 A local jug with dark-on-light floral motifs.

53 A local flower vase with light-on-dark floral motifs.

54 A local strainer with light-on-dark floral motifs.

55 An imported ewer with dark-on-light floral motifs.

56 An imported rhyton with dark-on-light floral motifs.

57 A local vase *(kymbe)* decorated with dolphins.

58 A local breasted ewer decorated with swallows.

59 A local ewer decorated with dolphins.

60 An offering table decorated with dolphins.

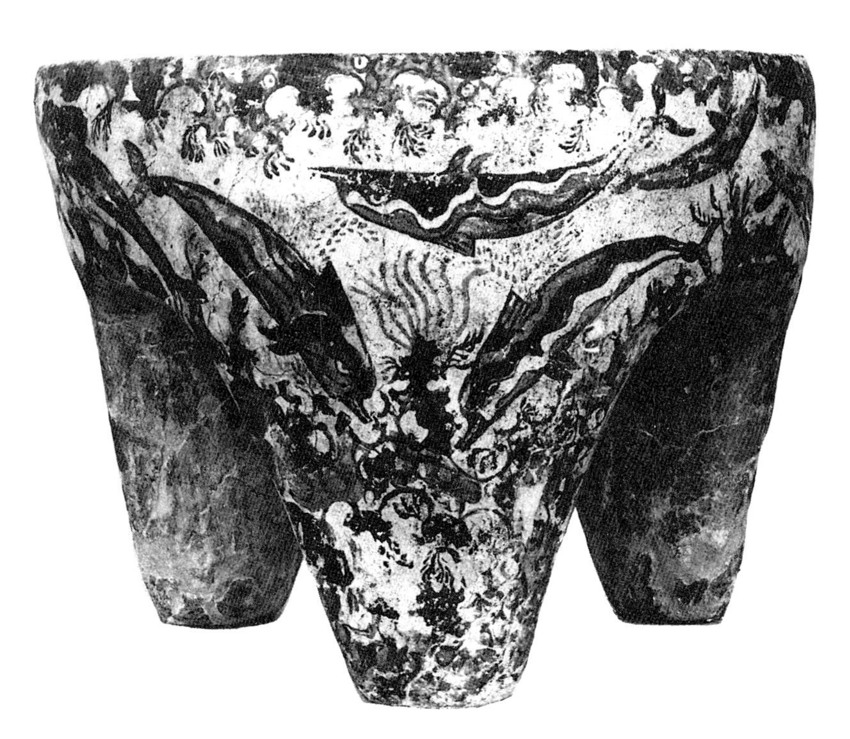

61 A local vase decorated with grapes.

62–63 Breasted ewers.

64 A clay 'barbecue'.

65 A marble vase.

Stone industry

66 A sealstone with a griffin.

67 A marble chalice.

68 A stone 'demolition ball' with grooves made for the ropes used to suspend it.

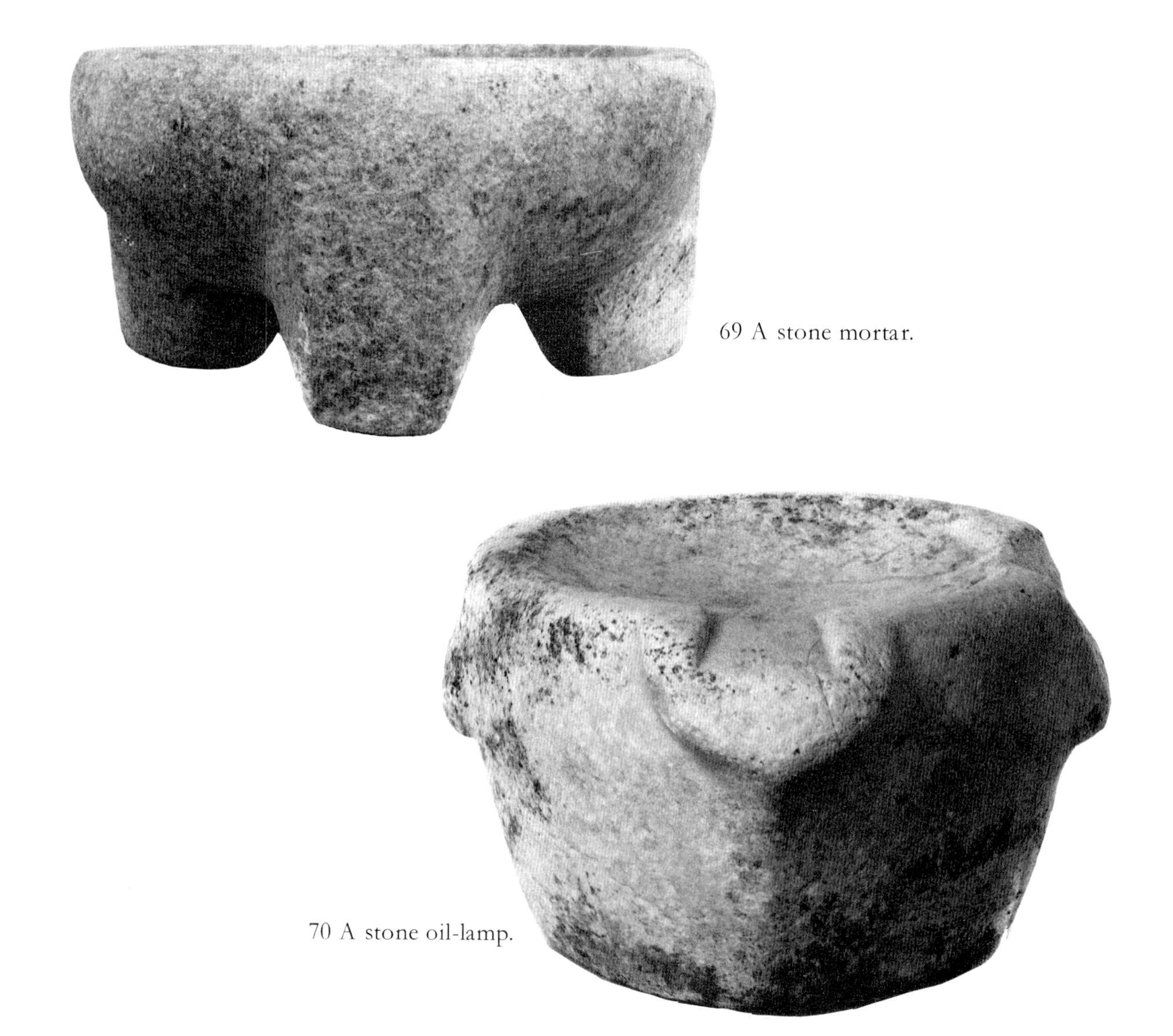

69 A stone mortar.

70 A stone oil-lamp.

71 A stone pestle and mortar.

72 A stone 'bird's nest' bowl.

Metallurgy

73 Lead balance weights.

74 Bronze tools and weapons. Above, left and right: various sickles. Above centre: two broken awls (with a knife to their immediate right). Bottom two rows: various daggers.

75–76 An undecorated bronze ewer and a reconstruction drawing of a decorated one.

77 Bronze scale pans.

78–80 *Top to bottom:* a bronze baking pan, spouted cup, and 'frying pan'.

Weaving

81 Lentoid clay loom weights, found in groups of several dozen with debris fallen from the upper storeys, which suggests that the loom was part of the furniture of the residential apartments in each house.

82 Impressions of matting on fragments of Middle Cycladic pottery.

83 The remains of a wicker basket, preserved in a cocoon of volcanic ash.

84 The cast of a small table, made by pouring liquid plaster-of-Paris into the void in the volcanic ash left by the disintegrated wooden original.

85 The base of a jar with snail-shells, probably imported from Crete as a luxury item.

painting to be enemy vessels, whilst the Theran ones should be in the missing part of the wall-painting.

Mrs A. Sakellariou, on the other hand, has rejected entirely the idea of the scenes being outside the Aegean as well as their interpretation as a battle. She interprets the painting as a scene from a sea festival in which armed men 'could be a guard of honour'; the bodies in the water are not drowned men or victims of a sea-battle, but are 'swimmers in a display of skill'.

Room 5 (upper frieze: east wall) A narrow frieze painted above the series of doors and niches depicts a landscape. On both banks of a meandering river wild beasts are shown amidst palm trees and other exotic plants and bushes. Predominant among the beasts is a griffin at a flying gallop; a spotted panther-like feline stalks a group of ducks and below the griffin there is a galloping deer. All the movement portrayed in the scene is in a left-right direction, except for a duck, behind the griffin, which flies towards the left. Perhaps the duck belongs to another faunal group orientated in the reverse direction. Both the flora and fauna in this riverscape led Marinatos to recognize a North African landscape, which further supported his Libyan theory.

plate XV

plate 29

Room 5 (upper frieze: south wall) The most impressive and informative painting from Akrotiri is the frieze which, from the site of its discovery, seems to have covered a narrow strip of the south wall above a series of niches. The general theme is the voyage of a flotilla from one harbour town and its arrival at another. The town from which the ships depart lies at the foot of a mountainous region from which a stream rises and encircles the town. The mountains are forested and there is a lion in pursuit of a herd of deer escaping towards the left. The town within the river's embrace consists of multi-storeyed houses. Small, isolated buildings are shown beyond the left branch of the river. Two men clad in animal skins are conversing beside the left branch of the river, while the rest of the population bid the vessels farewell, either from the flat roofs of the houses or from the quayside. The flotilla consists of eight sailing ships depicted in two rows, three above and five below. Due to the spatial limitations, only three vessels have their masts upright; in all the others the masts are lowered and supported by bifurcated poles. Only one of the lower row of vessels has its mast raised and this is the only ship in the composition shown in full sail. Six of the vessels have paddlers – nineteen or twenty-one pairs all facing towards the prow. The small boat below the town is propelled by five oarsmen facing the stern, while the fully rigged ship only uses its sails. That this ship moved faster than the others is also indicated by the fact that there are two steersmen–on all the others only one man is shown–and possibly by the flying birds (doves?) with which the vessel is decorated. Perhaps this relatively small ship was the messenger of the fleet? Its passengers are protected by a kind of parapet, exclusive to this vessel. The decoration on the other six vessels derives from the animal kingdom, showing lions and serpents in particular. On the largest ship, embellished with garlands or bunting, there is a combination of lions and dolphins. At the stern of each ship there is a special structure which looks like a

figs 20, 21
plate X

cabin, and houses a seated person (the captain?). The 'cabins' are identical to the much larger 'banners' which were painted on the walls of the adjacent Room 4. Since they are structurally independent from the actual vessels, they may be palanquins as was suggested for the 'banners'. Boar's-tusk helmets are often suspended from one of the 'cabin' poles as well as from the poles supporting the lowered sails.

The flotilla arrives at another harbour town with multi-storeyed houses. Small boats are stationed in two bays, and one of the boats, manned by two oarsmen, moves towards the incoming vessels. The town populace watches the arrival of the ships: a number of men have gathered along the seashore, while others watch from nearby hills, roof tops or large windows. The architecture of the town shows Minoan characteristics, as does the dress of its inhabitants. On one of the hills stands a complex of small buildings, perhaps a watchtower, towards which several men run.

This frieze has been interpreted in a variety of ways. Whether it represents the return of a fleet following a successful mission abroad, or whether it shows a ceremony of some kind or a visit by friends or allies is a matter for conjecture. The joyfulness of the picture, however, cannot be denied. Both the vessel festooned with decorations and the dolphins playing around the ships are indicative iconographic elements. Marinatos' proposal that the garlanded vessel was the flagship of the fleet and its captain the admiral and owner of the West House may have some validity crucial to the interpretation of the frieze. For the 'cabin' of the 'flagship' is identical to one of the 'banners' or 'screens' from the walls of Room 4–was this perhaps the palanquin of the owner of the West House?

Xesté 3

figs 5, 7

This building has produced the largest number of wall-paintings so far. Although they are still at an early stage of restoration, it can be estimated that they covered a total area of several dozen square metres. Many rooms in this building were decorated with murals and each room seems to have had a different subject. On the walls of the 'lustral basin' in the northeast corner of the building a wall-painting showed several women involved in what is even today an exclusively female task among the Akrotiri villagers–the gathering of crocus stamens for saffron. Each lady picks the precious stamens and puts them in a basket which is later emptied into a larger container, probably a basket too, placed in front of a large seated female figure. The seated female is flanked by a blue monkey on her right and a griffin on her left. Each woman wears a different dress, though coiffure and dresses are all in the Minoan style. The women are adorned with necklaces, earrings, bracelets and even anklets.

plates 30–32

The fact that this wall-painting was discovered in the 'lustral basin' suggests that it had a religious significance, but as yet one can give no more specific interpretation. The mural will undoubtedly prove an invaluable source of information, not only about a particular female activity in prehistoric Akrotiri, but also about hairstyles, jewelry, types of dress, fabric and embroidery etc. In addition,

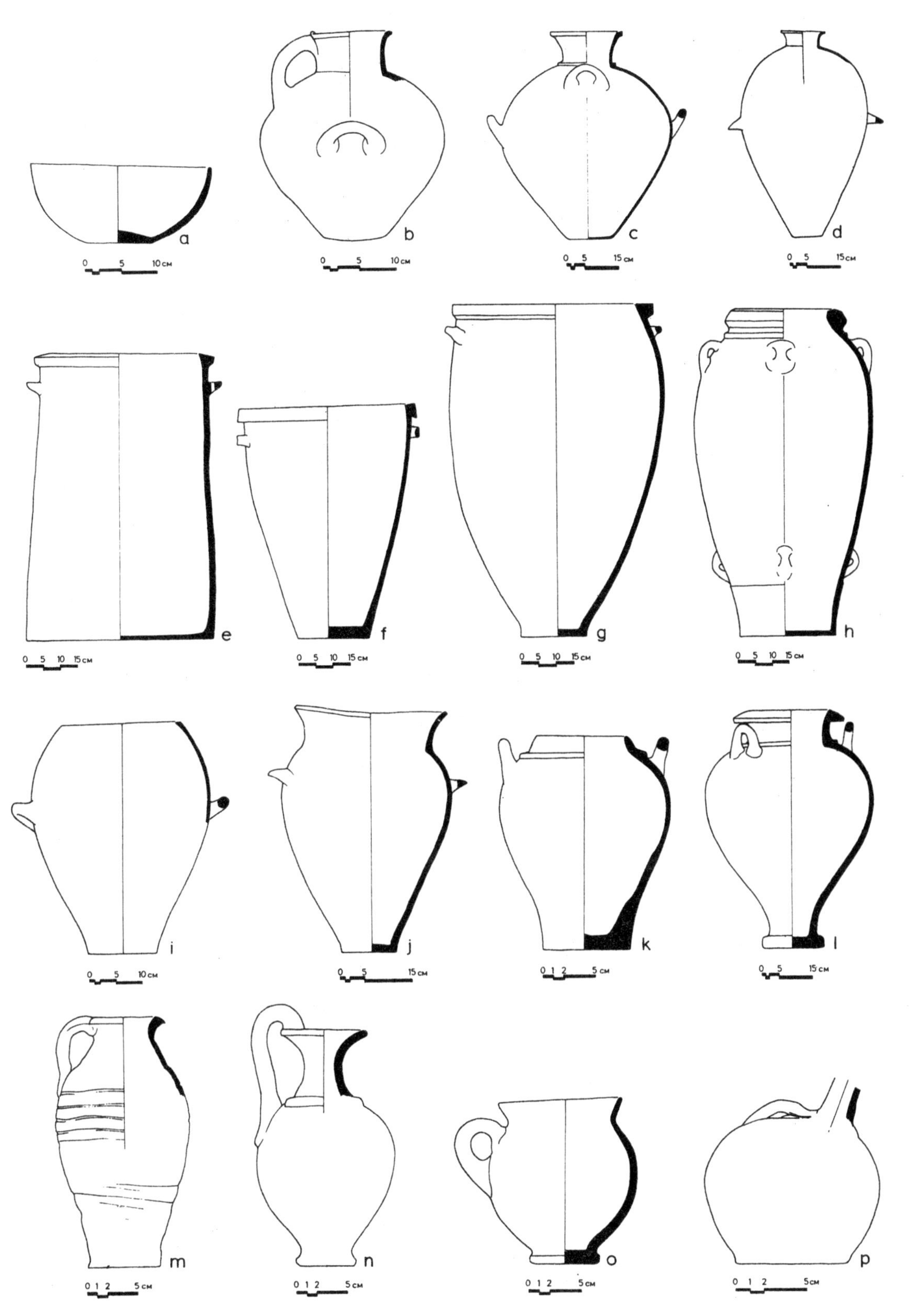

13 Middle and Late Cycladic pottery from Akrotiri: (a) Middle Cycladic bowl; (b) Middle Cycladic hydria; (c) Middle Cycladic krater; (d) Middle Cycladic amphorae; (e-l) various types of Late Cycladic jar; (m, n, o) Late Cycladic jugs; (p) Late Cycladic flask.

the freedom of movement to be observed in these figures constitutes further proof of the artistic independence of Akrotiri from the conventions of the Cretan palaces.

Despite their still fragmentary state, other compositions from Xesté 3 can be discerned including:

a) A second group of women performing an undefined action.

b) A frieze showing blue monkeys performing human activities, such as playing musical instruments, holding a sword etc.

c) Friezes with running spirals.

d) Relief bands in a diamond arrangement enclosing painted rosettes.

figs 13–15

Pottery

The excavations at Akrotiri have produced a large variety of artefacts revealing diverse aspects of Late Bronze Age technology.

Pottery is the commonest and most enduring commodity in the material culture of the majority of ancient societies, and for this reason is of great importance to the archaeologist. At Akrotiri pottery is particularly abundant because of the peculiar circumstances surrounding the demise of the town–its sudden evacuation meant that the inhabitants took only their valuable possessions with them–and because of the excellent conditions which preserved the artefacts generally. A large number of pottery vessels were stored in each building so far uncovered: today, therefore, we have several thousand more-or-less intact vases as well as innumerable sherds.

figs 13–15 Pottery vessels served a host of purposes and so tell us a great deal about the society which produced them. Large jars were used as containers for storage of goods (foodstuffs, liquids, clothing). Others (e.g. stirrup jars) were designed for the transportation of certain commodities. There were also vessels for preparing and cooking food, for eating and drinking and many other diverse activities (bath-tubs, braziers, oil-lamps, cult vessels, bee-hives, flower pots etc). Clearly the size, shape, fabric and perhaps the decoration of the vases were closely related to their use.

Technology

Various scientific analytical techniques have been applied to pottery fragments from Akrotiri (petrological, thin-sections, mineralogical, chemical etc.) and these have more or less confirmed the archaeologists' classification of the pottery, based on stylistic observations, as being of either local manufacture or imported. As one would expect, the bulk of the pottery found at Akrotiri is locally made. Furthermore, the indigenous pottery comes in a wider variety of shapes and sizes than the imported wares. Perhaps this is because the local potters produced vessels designed to cope with virtually all the needs of the populace–from small drinking cups and domestic vessels to large containers, bath-tubs and even ritual vases. Imported wares were, on the other hand, either brought to

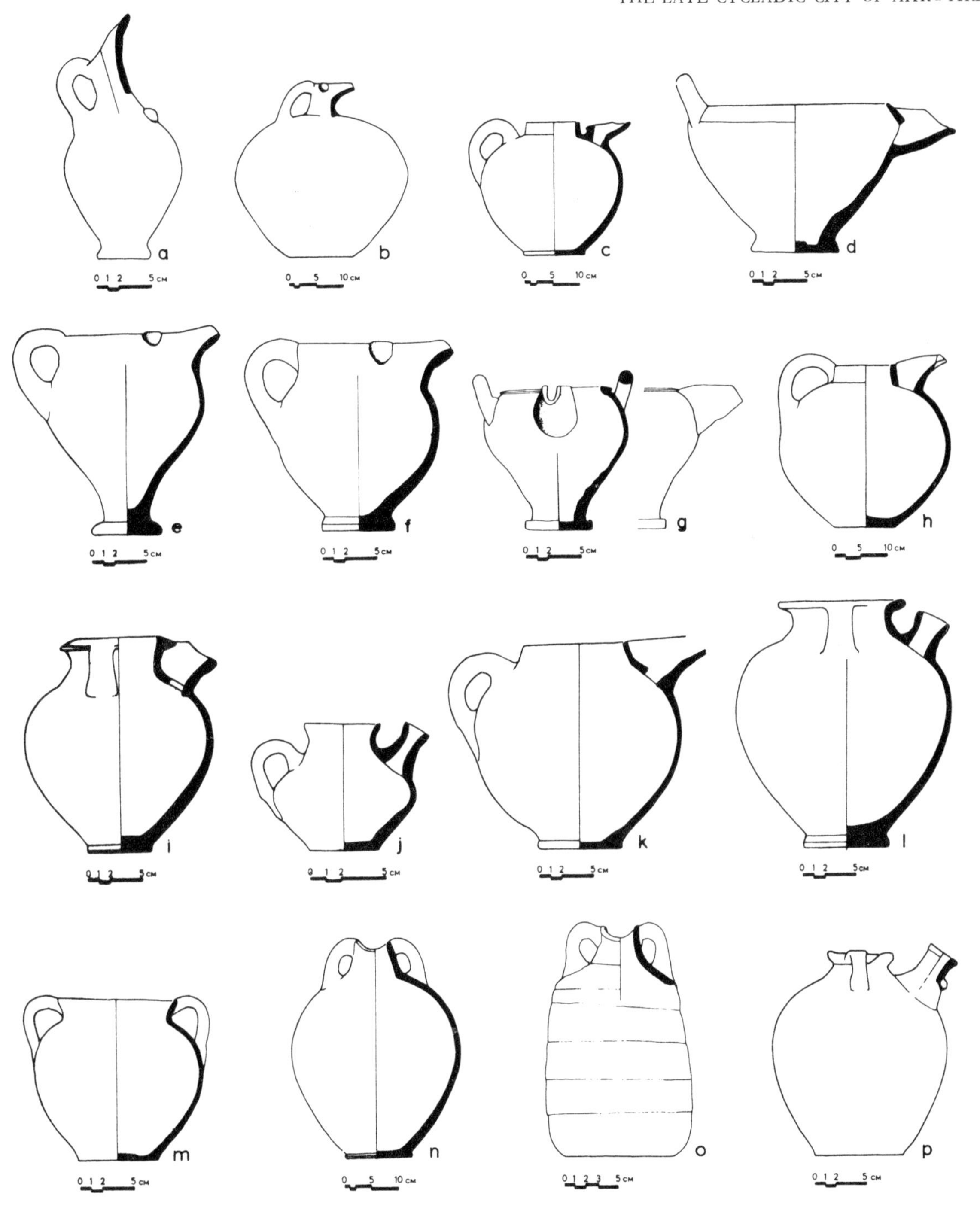

14 Late Cycladic pottery from Akrotiri: (a, b) ewers; (c) beak-spouted ewer; (d) bridge-spouted Cycladic bowl; (e, f) spouted jugs; (g) spouted amphora; (h) bridge-spouted jug; (i) bridge-spouted amphora; (j) feeding bottle; (k) bridge-spouted jug; (l) spouted amphora; (m, n, o) various amphorae; (p) stirrup jar.

Akrotiri as containers (particularly large containers) of other imported goods, or as specific 'luxury' items.

Locally made pottery is distinguished by its somewhat coarse fabric and buff-coloured clay. Analysis has shown that this clay contains pumice and inclusions of volcanic rocks. The local pottery of Akrotiri, unlike that from other Cycladic islands, is also characterized by the absence of mica. It is therefore suggested that the tripod cooking pots which have mica inclusions in their biscuit were either imported or made locally from imported clay. The reddish-brown appearance of the clay recalls that of Naxian pottery, and the tripod cooking pots may indeed be from the island of Naxos. Since mica imparts special heat-resistant qualities to the clay, the choice of such a clay for the manufacture of cooking vessels cannot have been fortuitous.

Forms

If one follows Furumark's definition of form as 'the way in which the vessel is executed according to the requirements of practical use', then more than fifty different pot types can be distinguished at Akrotiri–and this is by no means the final figure. Every season there are surprises and new forms are added to the repertoire. A selection of those known so far is presented in figs 13–15.

One category of vessels includes various types of *pithoi* (jars), designed for storage. One particular type of jar is provided with a spout at the base and was obviously intended to contain liquids. Bath-tubs have also been found in a secondary use for storing such produce as flour, cereals and legumes. Pouring vessels constitute another large category of vases at Akrotiri. The most characteristic types in this category are beak-spouted jugs, breasted or nippled ewers, bridge-spouted cups and *askoi* (flasks). A wide range of cups can be categorized as drinking vessels. To this category one may add the type of small vase with a tubular spout known as a 'feeding bottle'.

plates 47–52, 55, 58, 59, 61, 62, 63

Besides these broad categories of vessels there are smaller groups such as plant pots, fruit stands, strainers, tripod cooking pots, braziers or incense burners. Different types of rhytons (vases provided with a small pouring hole at the bottom) are generally described as libation vessels, but some of the conical funnels, found in large quantities in almost every house at Akrotiri, also belong to this class. Zoomorphic rhytons, such as those in the form of a bull, a triton shell, a lion's or a boar's head, certainly had a ritual function.

plates 43–46, 53, 54, 56, 57, 64

plates 39–41

Decoration

Very few vase forms seem to have been intended to remain undecorated (undecorated types include small conical cups, cooking pots, braziers, incense burners and in general those vessels whose function would spoil the decoration). In fact, even domestic pottery, including storage jars, was embellished with some kind of ornament.

plates 43–46

The old Cycladic tradition of incised decoration seems to have been abandoned, except for a very limited number of domestic wares. These include large

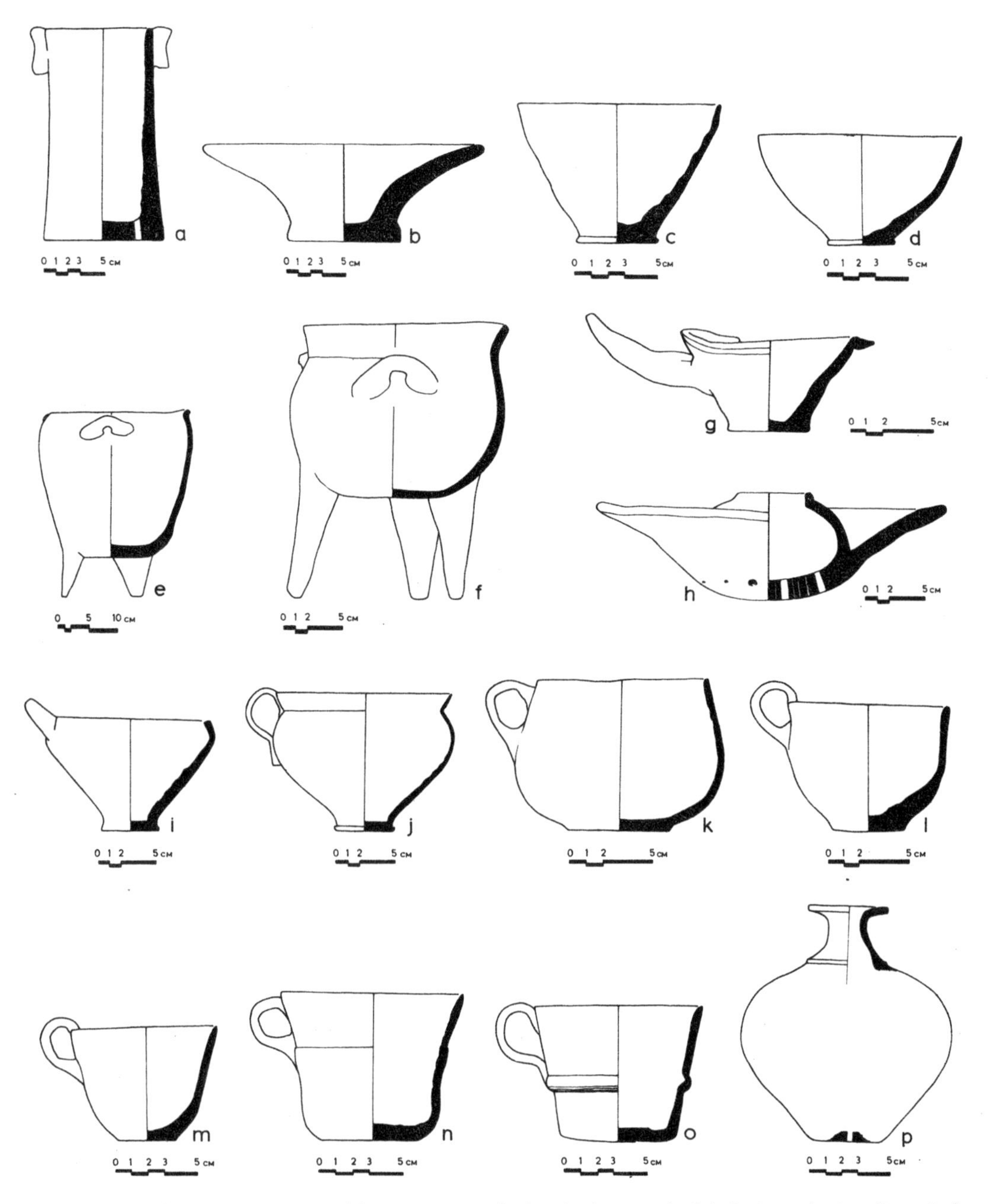

15 Late Cycladic pottery from Akrotiri: (a) cylindrical plant pot; (b) fruitstand; (c, d) conical cups; (e, f) cooking pots; (g, h) incense burners; (i) Cycladic bowl; (j-m) cups; (n, o) 'keftiu'-type cups; (p) rhyton.

ovoid storage jars to which horizontal bands of clay were applied to conceal the joins between the rings of clay of which the jar was made. Vertical striations were often incised on these bands.

Plastic decoration was commoner than incised, though its popularity was likewise restricted. It too occurs on storage jars, either as rows of small crescents applied over the junction bands or as a rope-like motif. Plastic knobs were also used as decorative elements and are found between the handles of jars and on either side of the spout in a category of beak-spouted ewer. In the latter case they were also painted in imitation of eyes.

Vases were most commonly decorated by painting. The principal colours used were black, brown and red, although intermediate shades came about as the result of firing. White was applied only to imported vases, on top of dark painted motifs, for accentuation or as a complementary element.

The arrangement of painted motifs on the pottery of Akrotiri follows two systems, each quite different from the other. One system follows the Cretan tradition of zonal syntax of decorative themes. The entire surface of the vase is divided into horizontal zones, broad or narrow, defined by horizontal bands. Within each zone the decoration consists of either a unitary pattern or a combination of motifs. The second system of decoration follows the Cycladic tradition in which the entire surface of the vase remains undivided and the motifs are freely arranged over it.

plates 47, 48

The decorative motifs applied in each of these two systems also follow the corresponding traditions. Geometric motifs are more popular in the Cretan pottery tradition, whereas pictorial elements have a long history in the Cycladic tradition. The repertoire of geometric designs consists mainly of linear motifs, such as horizontal bands, groups of vertical striations (tortoise shell), spirals or circles. Pictorial decoration is almost wholly restricted to vases produced locally. Its themes are usually taken from the plant and animal kingdoms, though the human figure is not entirely absent. Reeds or grasses, barley plants or ears, lilies, crocuses, myrtle and vetches represent the floral motifs on the Theran pottery, while from the animal kingdom the commonest motifs are fish, birds and wild goats. A notable Cycladic feature is the decoration of vessels with images of other vessels, especially the nippled ewer, which is often painted on other ewers or jars.

fig. 16

plates 49–59

Pottery vessels quite clearly fulfilled a vast range of requirements at Akrotiri, hence the enormous number of vases of local manufacture. Taking into account the standardization of types and the association of certain decorative motifs with particular forms, this would suggest production on an industrial scale. One gains the impression that there was somewhere a major centre where vases were manufactured to cover all the requirements of the city. Perhaps the potters themselves were organized into some kind of corporate body, such as a guild. Standardization did not, however, lead to slavish imitation, and the inventiveness of the Theran potters is apparent not only in the uniqueness of certain ceramic types but also in the originality of decoration, theme and syntax.

16 Decorative patterns on Akrotiri pottery.

Stone industry

plates 65–72

The Akrotiri excavations have produced large numbers of stone tools and vessels, despite the fact that the main period of occupation at the site was during the Late Bronze Age, when one might have expected metal tools to have supplanted stone ones. The anomaly may be explained by the abundance of suitable raw materials, native to the island. The products of the stone industry at Akrotiri fall into three categories: tools, vases and minor objects, including obsidian artefacts.

Grinders, pestles, polishers, hammers, anvils, millstones, demolition 'balls' (large hammerstones for demolishing walls) and anchors constitute the main types of stone tool or implement from Late Bronze Age Thera.

fig. 17

The stone vases from Akrotiri fall into two main categories: imported and locally made. According to Professor Peter Warren, the leading authority on Minoan stone vases, there was at Akrotiri a 'flourishing local industry in both local volcanic materials and fine imported stones'. In addition, other fine vases were imported from Crete and elsewhere. He has distinguished the following non-local materials among the stone vases at Akrotiri: alabaster, gypsum, several varieties of limestone and marble, *rosso antico* and serpentine. The different vase forms which occur in non-local stones include the *alabastron,* various types of bowl (bird's nest, blossom, spouted etc.), several kinds of jar, chalices, cups, oil-lamps, pithoi and rhytons. Despite the variety of distinct types, the number of imported vases is actually much smaller than of vases made of local stone. These latter examples are much coarser and were presumably destined for everyday use. They include various types of basin or tray, mortars, oil-lamps and a large pithos, all made from stones which are mainly of volcanic origin (trachyte, black lava, tuff).

In addition to some minor objects made of local stone a limited number of imported seals have also been found at Akrotiri, stressing the affinities of its culture with the Minoan/Mycenaean world.

Obsidian blades are not so common at Akrotiri, perhaps because stronger, longer and larger blades could be–and indeed were–manufactured from bronze. What is abundant, however, is obsidian in the form of chips or flakes. It is possible that ready-made obsidian flakes or blades were imported from Melos. But the discovery of a sizeable core of obsidian suggests that artefacts were also manufactured locally.

Metallurgy

Despite the scarcity of metal objects at Akrotiri, it is likely that the affluence of the site in the Late Cycladic I period can be attributed, in part, to the trade in metal ingots. Crete and Cyprus were the most important centres of metallurgy in the Late Bronze Age and Cycladic entrepreneurs seem to have operated as middlemen in the metals trade. Metal objects at Akrotiri were considered to be luxury items and may have been removed by the inhabitants when the city was

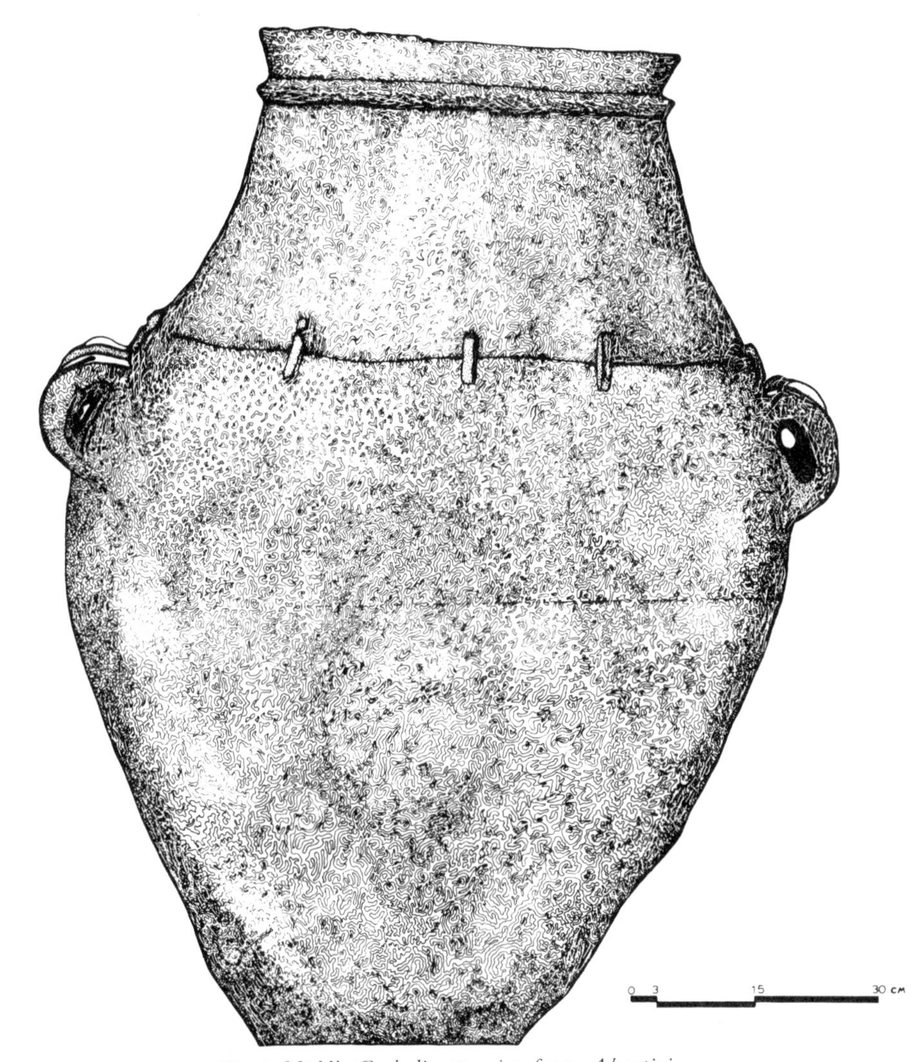

17 A Middle Cycladic stone jar from Akrotiri.

evacuated before the final eruption of the volcano. Occasionally, however, Late Bronze Age metal objects are found, especially those made of bronze and lead: silver and gold objects are practically non-existent. Among the bronze implements one should mention fish-hooks, knives, daggers, chisels, sickles and awls. Besides these, some vessels of bronze have been found, such as the pans from a pair of scales, braziers or incense burners, frying-pans, baking pans, tripod cooking pots, ewers and bowls.

plates 73–80

Lead at Akrotiri appears almost exclusively in the form of discoid balance weights. They occur in various sizes and so far they represent almost one third of the total number of Minoan lead weights known from the Aegean area. An object in the form of a cross, also of lead, was found in Room Delta 8.

plate 73

Of the few silver objects found, the small rings of thin silver wire from Room Delta 16 are the most important. Gold is not represented among the finds except for a minute fragment of thin gold leaf.

Furniture

The volcanic ash which covered the city of Akrotiri often penetrated into the houses in large quantities, and it is in these layers of fine volcanic dust that the 'negatives' of disintegrated wooden objects have been found well preserved. Using these negatives as moulds, liquid plaster-of-Paris can be poured in to produce casts of parts of, or even entire pieces of, furniture, such as beds, tables, chairs or stools. The cast of a small bed, 1.60 m long and 0.68 m wide, was retrieved in this way from Room Delta 2, as was a fragmented stool, whose subsequent reconstruction measured 42 x 28 cm and 38 cm in height. Casts of parts of similar stools and a chair have been salvaged from other areas in the excavation, but the most remarkable piece recovered was a round tripod table from the ground floor of Room Delta 1. Here the legs show signs of carved decoration. Small tripod 'offering tables' known from the Minoan world and from Akrotiri

plate 84, *fig. 18*

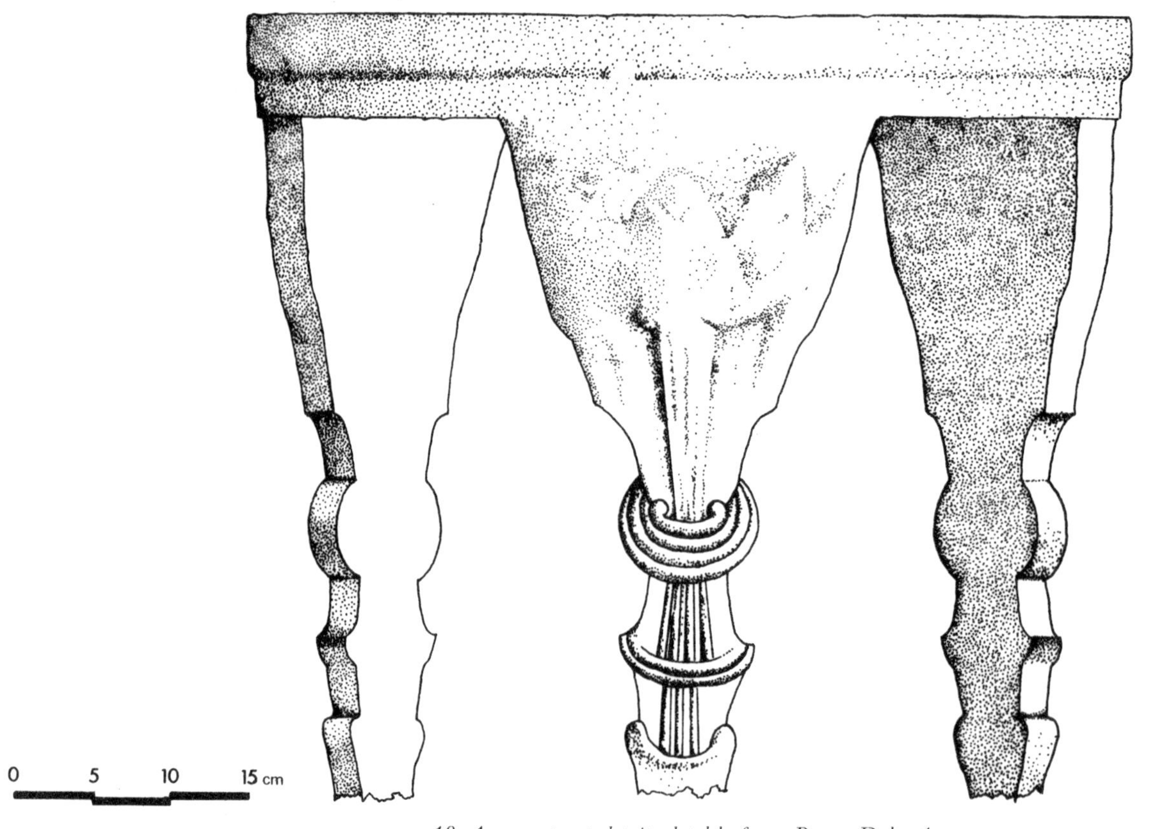

18 A reconstructed tripod table from Room Delta 1.

may be considered close cousins of this tripod table. 'Offering tables' from Akrotiri are either made of clay or coated with plaster, decorated in the same technique as the wall-paintings. Excellent examples of the plastered type are those decorated with dolphins. Among the pieces of furniture one should class a small stone stool found in a Middle Cycladic context.

Weaving

Evidence for weaving at Akrotiri is only indirect, because no remains of textiles have been found. The wall-paintings indicate fashions in male and female dress, but they do not tell us whether the materials used for clothing were locally made or not. The discovery, however, of crushed murex shells used secondarily to strengthen earthen floors suggests that dying of cloth (murex being the main source for red dye) was carried out at Akrotiri–and by implication, weaving too. More direct evidence comes from the lentoid clay objects found in large numbers among the ruins of almost every house. These are provided with suspension holes and must surely have served as loom-weights. They are found in groups of several dozen, mixed with debris fallen from the upper storey, which suggests that the loom was part of the furniture of the residential apartments in each house. It becomes evident, therefore, that weaving was a major feature of the domestic economy and occupied a large number of people, probably women. A surplus of cloth may have even been produced since it was needed not only for the very varied garments seen in the wall-paintings but also for sails and other items. Woollen yarn could have been spun from the fleeces of local sheep and goat, while flax for linen may have been grown on the island.

plate 81

Weaving and matting are closely allied. Mat impressions appear on Early Cycladic II pottery, at Akrotiri particularly on the bases of vases found in Early and Middle Cycladic contexts. It seems that mats were used either as slow-moving hand-operated tournets on which the pots were made or to put the vases on to allow them to dry after manufacture. It is interesting that mat impressions on pottery vases disappear with the advent of Late Cycladic I. For this period, however, evidence for matting is more direct. Remains of mats have been found in Room Delta 3 covering the bronze hoard, in the basement of Room 4 in the West House and elsewhere.

plate 82

Similar in technique to matting is basketry. Baskets, probably made of rush or wicker, are preserved (albeit in powdery condition) only if entirely covered with fine volcanic ash. Their preservation, removal from the dig and conservation is another achievement of the Greek restorers. One basket, probably made of wicker, was found in the Mill House of Sector Alpha with a quantity of sea-urchin shells and pins underneath it. Perhaps just before the disaster it had been suspended from the ceiling by the pins, and had contained these sea-urchins, freshly gathered from the shore. Other baskets, made of rush, were found in the basement of Room 4 in the West House, in the basement of Room Delta 1 and elsewhere.

plate 83

Subsistence

The Therans of Late Bronze Age Akrotiri practised animal husbandry as their forefathers had done, on the evidence of the large number of animal bones discovered at the site. Quantitative analyses indicate that sheep and goat were the primary source of meat (72 per cent of the bones), with pigs second (19 per cent) and cattle third (9 per cent). The lack of butchering marks on the cattle bones suggests that bovines were in fact raised as beasts of burden for ploughing, carrying and perhaps for milk rather than for meat. Game animals were also eaten, as is shown by the presence of boars' tusks among the food residues. Since it is most unlikely that boars were native to the island in Late Cycladic I times, one must assume that they were hunted elsewhere, perhaps on Crete or the Greek mainland, and brought as carcasses to Thera.

Animal husbandry seems to have been supplemented by sea-food. Besides fish, delicacies such as sea-urchins, limpets and tritons were not unknown to the Akrotirians (many of their shells have been found among the ruins or inside containers). Snails appear to have been most popular; quite large pithoi have been found containing white snail-shells. This particular species was probably not indigenous, but was common on Crete, so may have been imported from there as a luxury food in substantial quantities.

plate 85

From the carbonized remains of grains we know that the diet of the Akrotirians included various types of legumes, possibly lentils and split peas (fava). Bread was made from barley flour, as the remains of flour from Room Alpha 1 suggests and as the mill installations in each house also demonstrate. Olives were probably imported, while sesame and saffron could have been ingredients for cakes. Whether olive oil formed part of the diet or was used as an ointment is a matter for conjecture. We can be certain, however, that nuts–almonds and pistachios–were eaten since they were kept in jars. It is also possible that the Akrotirians enjoyed honey as well. Grapes are often depicted on the vases, so one can doubtless conclude that viticulture was practised.

fig. 19

Apart from eating the grapes, it seems very likely that the inhabitants of Akrotiri used them to make wine, storing it in large jars designed specifically for the purpose. As travellers and merchants they might also have come into contact with other, more exotic, drinks, such as beer, a well-known Egyptian beverage.

Trade and communication

plate X

Both the West House murals depicting the flotilla and the exotic animals in many of the paintings tend to suggest that Akrotiri had strong overseas contacts. A Late Cycladic I sailing ship would have been a sturdy vessel, capable of coping with the rough seas of the Aegean. The best-preserved (but not the largest) vessel of the flotilla shows nineteen paddlers in one row, with presumably another nineteen down the other side of the ship. In real life the space required for each paddler must have been about 70–80 cm, so the nineteen paddlers

figs 20, 21

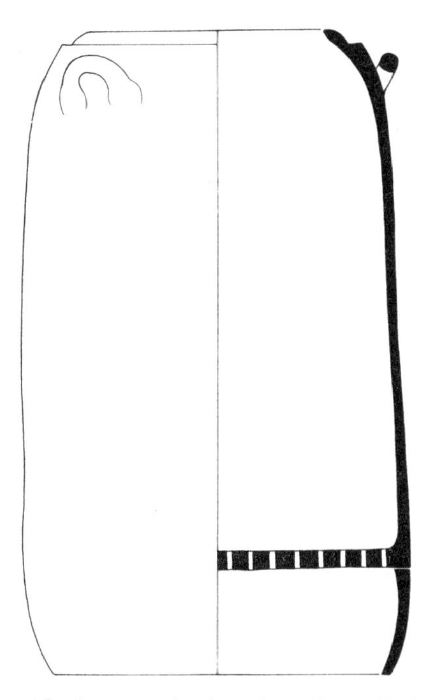

19 A pottery bee-hive from Room Delta 17, indicating that the Akrotirians kept bees for honey.

would together have taken up at least 13–15 m of the length of the ship. Assuming the drawing is to scale, the entire vessel would have been about 39–45 m long, since the paddlers occupy only one third of the total length of the ship. Seacraft of this size must have made voyages between the islands relatively easy.

The supposition that overseas trade was of vital importance to the Akrotirians is lent further weight by the evidence given above and below (chapters 2 and 5) that the Cycladic islanders probably had control of the Aegean seaways during the entire Bronze Age. It is also quite likely that they dominated trade between the Aegean and the eastern Mediterranean. The Akrotiri excavation itself confirms the close contacts maintained between Thera and the Greek mainland and Crete. Pottery from both these foreign lands is quite common, either as containers for other commodities (such as foodstuffs), or as wares traded in their own right. Professor Peter Warren has pointed out that more Cretan vases have been found at Akrotiri than at any other site, either on Crete or outside it, with the exception of Knossos.

Close links between Thera and the other Aegean islands are demonstrated by, among other things, the import of huge quantities of obsidian from Melos. Connections with the eastern Mediterranean become equally evident when one looks at, for instance, the vases made of gypsum which Professor Warren believes must be of Syro-Palestinian origin, or the Syrian amphora found in Room Delta 9.1. Perhaps the amphora was imported full of beer or grains, as Mrs K. Thorpe-Scholes has suggested. Two ostrich-egg-and-faience rhytons

plate 42

20 A detail of the 'Flotilla fresco in Room 5 of the West House. Ships are shown leaving a harbour.

found in Room Delta 16 imply contacts with Egypt, even if the transformation of the eggshells into rhytons was–as Marinatos proposed–'due to Aegean workmanship'.

Silver and lead were probably imported from Laurion, on the east coast of Attica, or from the island of Siphnos. Bronze vases and implements share characteristics with Creto-Mycenaean examples and may have been imported from Crete or the Greek mainland. The excavations at Akrotiri also show that Thera was a production centre for tripod mortars made of local dacite; large numbers of these were exported to Crete.

Besides goods which endure long enough for archaeologists to excavate them, there must have been a considerable trade in commodities of a more perishable nature. For instance, Thera may have exported saffron, wine and honey and imported olive oil, olives, textiles and timber.

Writing and counting

Though the so-called potters' marks found incised on many Middle Cycladic vases are considered by some scholars to be symbols of a kind of communication throughout the Aegean, it is too early to speak of 'writing' in the Cyclades. This seems to have been the greatest contribution of Minoan Crete to the

Aegean world. The syllabic script system called 'Linear A' by Sir Arthur Evans was probably invented at Phaistos in the early centuries of the Middle Minoan period. From there it spread rapidly throughout Crete and near the end of the period was already in use in other Aegean islands. Fragments of clay tablets with Linear A writing have been found at Ayia Irini on Kea as well as at Phylakopi on Melos. No such tablets have been found so far at Akrotiri, but there is strong evidence that Thera too had already entered the cultural sphere of Crete. A few sherds found among the ruins bear signs in the Linear A script and, more importantly, a complete Linear A inscription was recovered on the shoulder of a large ewer found in Room Delta 4. This inscription comprises four signs which read *a-re-sa-na,* perhaps the name of a person or a place-name declaring the provenance of the ewer's contents.

More explicit is the use of the Minoan metric system in Thera as well as in the rest of the Aegean. Discoid Minoan lead weights have been found in considerable numbers and in various sizes. K. Petruso, who has studied them, has pointed out that the 'commonest ratio between any two adjacent denominations in the system is 1:2'. Some of these weights are marked with symbols which denote the factors or multiples of a unit which has been proved to be about 61 grams. The application of this metric system by the Akrotirians and the discovery of so many balance weights at Akrotiri–according to Petruso, Akrotiri and

plate 73

21 Another detail of the 'Flotilla' fresco, this time of the central section. The best-preserved ship in the group can be seen at the top.

Ayia Irini have yielded 'fully two thirds of the total number of Minoan balance weights known'–demonstrate not only the influence of Crete on Thera; they also bear witness to Akrotiri's importance as an Aegean commercial station.

Society

In the absence of written records it is difficult to reconstruct the social organization of Late Cycladic Akrotiri. The prehistorian, of necessity, relies on material remains which provide only a partial record. Usually, however, there are burials and offerings which shed light on social status and religious beliefs and practices. Unfortunately at Akrotiri the cemetery has not yet been found and so what follows must be considered an interim assessment of Theran society.

Objects made of precious materials–clues to the social and economic status of their owners–are also absent from the known material culture of Akrotiri. The townsfolk clearly had time before the impending disaster to flee their homes, taking with them most of their valuables. What remains for the archaeologist is the layout of the town and its architecture, its artistic legacy of wall-paintings, and the diverse artefacts discussed in the previous sections. From these some inferences about the people of Akrotiri can be drawn.

In previous chapters it has been demonstrated that the Late Cycladic I city of Akrotiri was not a newly founded settlement, but developed in this form during

the Middle Cycladic period, though its origins go back to the Early Bronze Age. Since no break in this one-thousand-year-long development has been observed, it is natural to suggest that most of the population was indigenous. The strong Minoan influence which is apparent in art and architecture has led some scholars to infer that Akrotiri was colonized by Late Minoan settlers. But the so-called Minoanization seems to be a superficial characteristic. Despite the copying of Minoan forms on some vases fashioned by the Akrotiri potters, the decoration applied on them, both in syntax and motifs, is entirely of Cycladic inspiration. The zonal arrangement typical of the decoration on Minoan vases tends to be abandoned in the Cyclades–and at Akrotiri–where a freer disposition of motifs is preferred. Moreover, the geometric or linear patterns, familiar on Late Minoan Ia vases, are less common in the Cyclades–and at Akrotiri–where pictorial motifs are more popular. The preference for themes from the animal kingdom is another Cycladic feature, almost unknown in Crete. One can make similar remarks about the wall-paintings which, despite their Minoan technique, show greater freedom than the more conventional Cretan art. The naturalistic approach of the Theran frescoes is closer to the spirit of Cycladic art. Taken together these observations lead one to suggest that Akrotiri was inhabited by an indigenous–Cycladic–population. But of course there may also have been small minorities, mainly from Crete and the Greek mainland.

fig. 16

Compared with contemporary settlements and considering the small size of the island, the conurbation at Akrotiri was very large and sufficiently organized to be called a town or city. So far over four acres have been excavated, within which large two-, three-, and four-storeyed buildings have been uncovered. These were either the dwellings of an affluent class, in which case the houses of poorer folk will presumably be found in peripheral zones; or they were multi-storeyed because there was a shortage of available building land. In either event, it emerges that the population of the town must have been quite large and tightly packed since there are very few open spaces suitable for squares. In this respect Akrotiri bears some resemblance to the towns of medieval Europe.

From the town plan and architecture it is clear that the community was highly organized. Streets were paved and beneath them ran drains carrying away domestic effluent. In order to keep buildings in good repair there must have been some sort of central municipal authority. Further evidence for this is provided by the large-scale engineering works undertaken after the earthquakes preceding the eruption. The streets were cleared of rubble and dangerous walls demolished so that the town could return to normality. It seems unlikely that this overall authority was vested in a single person, a ruler or king (as in the Minoan palaces of Crete), because none of the buildings excavated so far seems to have the right dimensions or internal arrangement for a palace–all the structures are private houses, comfortable residences of apparently large (possibly extended) families. That the whole community was an urban one is confirmed by the fact that there was no provision for the accommodation of animals within either the houses or the town as a whole. Ancillary and subsidiary rooms in the houses were for storage or use as workshops.

The wall-paintings of Akrotiri give us some insight into the nature of Theran society. The fact that they have been found in all the buildings uncovered to date implies that an appreciable sector of society was both familiar with them and could afford them. The art, as has been pointed out elsewhere, is Minoan from the point of view of technique. The artists, however, seem to have been free from the conventions of the Cretan palaces, and their work is more akin to folk art, originality and individuality being the keynote. Akrotiri society must, moreover, have been sufficiently civilized and differentiated to support a special class of painters: the murals are too abundant, varied in quality of execution and diverse in content to have been executed by a couple of amateur artists. Professor Schachermeyr has pointed out that at Akrotiri there was 'no court art, because there was no court and no conventions. Artists of various styles came together and, according to the various individual residences, they received different orders'.

Craftsmen too must have constituted specialized groups. Architects, masons and carpenters solved many of the highly sophisticated structural problems evident in the architecture of some of the houses. Potters, as we have seen, worked on an almost 'industrial' scale to satisfy local demand. Although neither potters' workshops nor kilns have been found within the excavated area, there is strong evidence that the bulk of the pottery unearthed was manufactured locally. Indeed the technique, repertoire of shapes and decoration, fabric and firing exhibit a degree of uniformity indicative of one main centre of production.

The lapidaries too must have been a specialized body of craftsmen. We have seen from the study of the stone industry that at least one kind of vessel–the tripod dacitic mortar–was produced on Thera and exported in considerable numbers. In fact, the stone tools, implements and vessels played such an important role in the everyday life of the Akrotirians that their production–like that of pottery–must have been on an 'industrial' scale.

There is neither direct nor indirect evidence that shipbuilding was carried out on Thera itself. However, the evidence of trade and communication as well as the long Cycladic tradition in seafaring suggests that it was a skill developed very early in these islands. A whole host of different craftsmen would have been involved: carpenters, shipwrights, riggers, sailmakers and many others.

There were, then, at ancient Akrotiri specialized groups of artists and craftsmen, in addition to the farmers and fishermen who provided basic subsistence for the inhabitants. But the way in which these specialized classes were organized, their terms of recruitment and their internal organization are all a matter of guesswork–there may, for example, have been guilds but we cannot be sure. Nor do we know the economic and status ranking of the craftsmen, or how they interacted with those requiring their goods or services–did such patron-client relations involve 'financial' transactions, for instance?

Although there is no direct evidence about religious beliefs at prehistoric Akrotiri, some information can be extracted from the architecture, the art and various artefacts. The religious character of what is known in Minoan architecture as a 'lustral basin' has generally been accepted. Such an installation–an oblong room accessible by a flight of steps–was found in the basement of Xesté 3, and provides the only undisputed architectural feature of religious character on the site. The discovery of a pair of stone 'horns of consecration' also suggests a religious character for the east wing of Sector Delta. Taken together with the presence of vessels commonly accepted as ritual objects–like the various types of rhytons and 'offering tables'–the 'lustral basin' and 'horns of consecration' seem to indicate a religion similar to, if not the same as, that practised in Minoan Crete. From some of the wall-paintings one can conjecture the kind of rituals or festivals in which the Akrotirians may have participated. Although still obscure, the probability that the female figures from the House of the Ladies belong to a religious scene has already been pointed out. It has also been suggested that the wall-painting of the Lilies in Room Delta 2 is connected with some great spring festival. Perhaps scenes from an autumn festival are depicted on the walls of the 'lustral basin' of Xesté 3; the character of this room leaves little doubt that the 'Saffron-gathering Ladies' are engaged in ritual activity.

In conclusion one can say that the religion–or at least the ritual–of the Akrotirians seems to have been the same as that practised in Crete, reflecting the high degree of cultural influence exercised by the Minoans over the population of the Cycladic islands.

5 Thera and the Aegean in the Late Bronze Age

The Minoan expansion in the Aegean

The Early Minoan settlement at Kastri on the island of Kythera is the oldest Cretan colony to have been found so far. But Crete's contacts with the outside world must have been forged much earlier. Melian obsidian, for instance, was imported to the island as early as the sixth millennium BC, in the Neolithic period. We know that these contacts intensified during the Early Bronze Age, but so far the only archaeological evidence is of Cycladic exports to Crete (obsidian, pottery, marble figurines); no proof has been found of Early Minoan exports to the Cyclades, though they may have been in the form of perishable materials or commodities (timber, clothes, wool and other items). The earliest known Cretan pottery found overseas consists of fragments of Kamares ware. Middle Minoan II and III pottery has been discovered in Melos, Kea, Delos, Thera, Naxos, Aegina, Paros, Amorgos, Lerna and Kythera. In the wider Aegean region similar pottery finds are attested at Miletus, Alisar Hűyűk, Boghazkőy and Iasos in Asia Minor, as well as on the island of Kos. Further south and east, Middle Minoan products reached Syria, Cyprus and Egypt. Their discovery in the eastern Mediterranean provides incontestable proof that communications were already well established between this region and the Aegean in the first half of the second millennium BC. But the presence of Minoan finds cannot be taken as evidence of the existence of Minoan settlements in these lands. Nor do they prove that Middle Minoan merchants 'established enclaves within existing settlements', as has been suggested. Middle Minoan products may not even have been conveyed in Minoan ships.

The picture is quite different in the Late Bronze Age, and the archaeological and literary evidence for a Minoan presence in the Aegean far more substantial. In Homer's *Iliad* (III: 230–33) Helen says that Menelaus in Sparta had offered hospitality to Idomeneus who visited him from Crete. From the Homeric hymn to Demeter we learn that the goddess reached Thorikos after a troubled journey from Crete (*Iliad* III: 123–26). According to the hymn to Apollo, Cretans from Knossos came via Pylos to Krissa (near Delphi: 469-72). Cretans led by Sarpedon, Minos' brother, are reported as having founded Miletus in Asia Minor. One of the earliest names for Rhodes was Telchinis, given to the island by the Telchines who arrived there from Crete via Cyprus. The many legends connected with Minos' personality indirectly suggest contacts between Crete and other places near and far. For example, Minos is reputed to have invaded Attica to avenge the death of his son Androgeos and as a consequence the Athenians were forced to pay tribute to Crete every nine years, sending seven youths and seven maidens to feed the Minotaur. The western Mediterranean region is associated with the end of Minos' life. According to tradition, in an attempt to catch Daedalus, Minos went to Sicily where he met his death and was subsequently buried.

In addition to the legends connecting Crete with its Mediterranean neighbours, there are also a number of Cretan trading stations given the name 'Minoa'. One is reported to have existed in the Gulf of Mirabello and another in the Bay of Souda, both in Crete. Outside Crete a Minoa is reported to have existed at Epidaurus Limera (present-day Monemvasia), on the Laconian coast of the Peloponnese. An islet off Megara in the Saronic Gulf was also called Minoa, as was one of the three Archaic cities on the island of Amorgos. Other cities with this name are said to have existed on Siphnos and Paros, and on Delos the name was given to one of the fountains. In fact, according to Apollonius of Rhodes, some of the Cyclades were called Minoan islands. But the toponym 'Minoa' was not restricted solely to the Aegean. One is reported on the Syrian coast, near Gaza, and another in Arabia, whilst in the western Mediterranean there was a Minoa on Corfu and another on the south coast of Sicily.

Most of the places which legend or tradition connect with Crete have, in fact, produced archaeological evidence of some contacts with the island from as early as the Middle Minoan period. It must be emphasized, however, that this evidence does not prove a Minoan influence over these places, let alone the existence of Minoan colonies.

Archaeological excavations have shown that the pronounced Minoan presence in the Aegean coincides with the first phase of the Late Minoan I period (1550–1500 BC). So marked is this presence at three major sites in the Cyclades that some scholars speak of their 'Minoanization'. At Phylakopi, Ayia Irini and Akrotiri Cretan influence is apparent in art, architecture, pottery, metalwork and other aspects of life. A Late Minoan I settlement was definitely founded at Ialysos (Trianda) on Rhodes before the Mycenaeans appeared on the island; but, apart from Kastri on Kythera, this is the only site outside Crete which is irrefutably Minoan and can be considered to have been a true Minoan colony. Thus a re-evaluation is needed of the references in the ancient sources to the Minoan thalassocracy and the colonization of the Cyclades by the Minoans.

The Cyclades in the Late Bronze Age I period

We have just noted that Minoan influence in the Aegean spread during the Late Minoan I period, as is shown particularly at Ayia Irini on Kea, Phylakopi on Melos and at Akrotiri. At all three sites, however, there is a strong continuity with earlier periods: the entire sequence of development of Cycladic civilization can be seen without a break, from as far back as the Early Bronze Age. In Phylakopi city III, despite some Minoan features in the architecture (e.g. the use of pillars), despite the presence of fragments of wall-paintings and the predominance of Minoan pottery forms and motifs, the character of the settlement is still indisputably Cycladic. As Furumark has pointed out, architecture and some types of domestic pottery suggest the continuation of native culture. He interprets the cessation of production of local decorated ware, which flourished previously, as signifying that Melos 'was now under Minoan rule, though still inhabited by a population of the old stock'.

In Late Cycladic I Ayia Irini the coexistence of Late Helladic I and Late Minoan IA pottery is not sufficient to erase the local character of the settlement since, according to J. Davies, 'local styles continued to be popular and there were no changes in techniques'. The importance of Ayia Irini in the extraction of silver, by virtue of its proximity to the mines of Laurium, helps explain its somewhat cosmopolitan character, as revealed by its material culture. This might also be the reason for the application of certain Minoan bureaucratic methods in administering the city's economy, such as the metric system of reckoning and writing.

The same picture has emerged from the city of Akrotiri on Thera. The Minoan influence, apparent in the architecture, pottery and wall-paintings, seems to have been manifested in traits which overlaid, but did not displace, local techniques and traditions.

From these three major sites, therefore, a general picture emerges which seems to be applicable to the rest of the Cyclades: on architectural and artefactual evidence Late Cycladic culture is a natural continuation of Middle Cycladic. Foreign influences, either Minoan or Helladic, left their mark, but the character of indigenous culture was never substantially altered. During the same period, the islands became foci of contact between the various civilizations peripheral to them, in particular those of Crete and the Greek mainland.

Late Cycladic I Thera

The flourishing city of Akrotiri was not the only settlement on Thera in the sixteenth century BC. Though not a large island, during Late Cycladic I times Thera seems to have been been quite densely populated. Several Late Cycladic I sites have been located, mostly during quarrying, but few have been properly excavated. The sites are usually represented by scanty architectural remains and pottery fragments. Most seem to have been either small country houses with animal pens, or satellite hamlets around the major city of Akrotiri.

In many ways it is unfortunate that much of the evidence about the distribution of prehistoric settlements on Thera should come from quarries (where one can reach the ancient levels without too much difficulty). The bulldozers that excavate the volcanic tephra can destroy all the ancient remains unless the quarry owner and his staff take an enlightened attitude towards the preservation of the history beneath their feet. Moreover the location of the quarry sites around the cliffs of the caldera–the tephra deposits are thicker here and easier to remove–inevitably leads to distortion in the known pattern of settlement on prehistoric Thera. Perhaps, however, this picture is not too inaccurate, since the configuration of the ground suggests a similar pattern.

Despite the sampling problems, it is clear that the southwest part of Thera was more densely populated than the north in Late Cycladic I times, just before the eruption of about 1500 BC. Even from the present lie of the land it is clear that prior to the eruption most of the northeast of the island was mountainous and unsuitable for agriculture–its present flat areas mainly result from the deposition of Late Cycladic I tephra which enlarged the island towards the sea. The region of Oia was the flattest area in the north and the site in the Oia quarry seems to have been the most important north-facing prehistoric settlement on Thera: located not far from the coast, it was probably the main point of contact between Thera and the neighbouring island of Ios.

fig. 1

Before the eruption of 1500 BC, the southwest region of Thera was undoubtedly the flattest terrain on the island, and most suitable for agriculture. Moreover, even if the height of the volcano was not, as some experts claim, of the order of 1,800 m, the southwest region would still have been in the lee of the volcano, sheltered from the cold northerly winds and perhaps receiving more rain than the rest of the island. The region thus had a double advantage: it guaranteed safe shelter for ships and encouraged the early ripening of crops. Indeed, one can expect other Late Cycladic I sites to be revealed here in the future.

Thera, the Cyclades and the Minoan thalassocracy

The pronounced Minoan influence apparent in Late Cycladic I architecture, material culture and art has often been regarded as a validation of the ancient belief that the Cyclades were Minoan colonies. But, as we have seen, Minoan influence was exercised over an indigenous population with its own distinctive culture.

The view that the Cycladic islands were colonized by King Minos was first expressed by Herodotus (1:171; 3:122). Thucydides later supported the theory, considering the colonization to be the first political fact in Greek history. King Minos, these historians explained, was attempting to rid the seas of piracy, but since the pirates were Carians and Lelegians, inhabitants of the Cyclades, the islands themselves had to be conquered. In reality, however, the story does not seem to have been quite so simple. From the archaeological evidence it becomes clear that the Cyclades were infiltrated gradually rather than swiftly colonized. No doubt Herodotus and Thucydides interpreted genuine information about this infiltration–blurred and distorted by time–in the idiom of their day, when colonization was common practice. But colonies are usually founded because of political unrest, religious dissent or economic strife at home, none of which seem to have been evident in Minoan Crete. Agricultural self-sufficiency must always have reduced possible tensions within the island. This has been confirmed by the archaeological evidence. No Middle or Late Minoan I settlements were fortified and no weapons were buried as grave goods. The serene character of Minoan art supports the image of a peaceful society, at one with itself, which would have had little impetus to send out colonizing war parties. The Cyclades, in any case, did not offer an abundance of fertile land, nor were the main Cycladic raw materials, such as marble and obsidian, in great demand during Late Minoan times.

If one turns to the evidence from the Cyclades themselves, the case against Minoan colonization is equally strong. The prosperity of sites such as Phylakopi, Ayia Irini and Akrotiri was not based on agriculture alone, nor can it be accepted that the art of Akrotiri was created by a simple farming society. Trade would have been the lifeblood of these communities from earliest times. Furumark, discussing Aegean history in this period, has pointed out that 'the islanders must have been sailors from the very beginning, and it is probable that the earlier Cycladic connections with Crete were largely due to their activity'. He also explains the lack of Cretan imports to Middle Helladic Greece as being due to the 'preponderance of Cycladic trade and shipping in the Aegean area'. It seems that Crete accepted this 'preponderance', which continued during the Late Cycladic I (Late Minoan IA) period also. Scholars dealing with the southern shores of the Mediterranean tend to confirm this assumption. R. S. Merillees, discussing Aegean Bronze Age connections with Egypt, has pointed out that 'the Minoans were in indirect [i.e. not direct] contact with Egypt during Dynasty XVIIIA and were supplanted by the Mycenaeans during the reign of Queen Hatshepsut'. The accepted chronology of Dynasty XVIIIA (*c.* 1550–1473 BC) more or less coincides with the Late Cycladic I period. Queen Hatshepsut reigned immediately after (1473–1458 BC). The agents of this indirect contact between Crete and Egypt during the Late Cycladic I period could very well have been the self-same Cycladic islanders in whose hands lay trade and shipping in the Aegean. Merillees may be correct in suggesting that the later mention in Egyptian sources of people from the 'Isles in the Midst of the Sea' refers to Mycenaean trading with Egypt. But the 'Isles in the Midst of the Sea', which constituted the western boundary of Tuthmosis III's sphere of influence, could well have been the Cyclades.

It can be argued that the idea of a Cycladic control of trade is untenable since no Cycladic objects have been found in places in the eastern Mediterranean where contacts with the Aegean have been attested. This is not an insurmountable objection, however, since, as has been said in a previous chapter, the Cyclades did not at that time produce anything durable which was in demand in foreign markets. The countries producing exportable commodities were Crete and, later, Mycenaean Greece. It is proposed here that these Cretan and Mycenaean products were conveyed in Cycladic vessels, for the islanders had centuries of experience in the construction and navigation of large sailing ships capable of voyaging to far-off lands. This would have been the reason why King Minos needed the islands: for the maritime skills of the inhabitants. Herodotus, the 'father of history', does in fact relate that Minos manned his ships with islanders. And in order to do so Minos had to conquer their hearts rather than their land. In this way he gained for himself not only transport for his expanding trade with the east, but also a defensive zone protecting Crete from attack from the north. The islanders would have had a vested interest in cooperation with Crete and been willing to defend their land while protecting Crete too.

If such a symbiotic relationship did indeed develop then a number of questions can be answered. Late Cycladic prosperity can be accounted for by thriving trade. The artistic independence of the islanders may be attributed to the degree of cultural and political autonomy they enjoyed. And the colonies which Thucydides reports were founded in the Cyclades by King Minos may be better understood as diplomatic missions despatched from Crete to secure the friendship and services of the islanders. Perhaps the leaders of these missions were members of the Cretan nobility, which would accord with Thucydides, who says that Minos sent his own sons to found the colonies on the islands.

If, as seems likely, the Cyclades played this intermediary role, then new light is shed on the way in which the thalassocracy of Minoan Crete–the control of the seas–operated. This control does not seem to have been military, backed by the force of arms. It was, rather, an economic control effected by trading with distant lands with the assistance or intervention of the Cycladic islanders. Maintenance of such a delicate, flexible system must have been difficult. Crete would have been most anxious to sustain amicable relations with her northern neighbours, who no doubt made ever-increasing demands as the process of Minoanization of their way of life advanced. In fact the end of the Minoan thalassocracy probably coincided with the Cretans' loss of control over the islands.

Mycenaeans on Thera?

Thera's splendid acme was achieved in the Late Cycladic I period, which is contemporary with the shaft graves of Mycenae. Ever since Schliemann's discovery of these royal graves in Circle A at Mycenae, with their unprecedentedly rich finds, scholars have argued endlessly over the provenance of the gold and the art. The questions posed have not really been satisfactorily answered. Professor Emily Vermeule delivered a series of lectures on the subject, summarizing the existing theories and proposing other possibilities. After pointing out that no similar artistic tradition existed in Middle Helladic Greece, she suggested that 'perhaps some of the craftsmen were trained elsewhere, presumably in Crete or possibly in the Cycladic islands, and to some degree good objects from other cultures were available to all of them for inspection.' She then proceeded to discuss various possible foreign influences on the art of the shaft graves, and remarked that 'the Cyclades, too, will surely prove more influential than we now know, especially perhaps for Grave Circle B'.

Some art objects from the excavations at Akrotiri closely resemble those from the shaft graves of Mycenae. The so-called leatherware jugs found in Melos,

Thera and Mycenae suggest close contacts between the Cyclades and the mainland, and analysis of their clay has demonstrated their non-Cycladic provenance. On the other hand, the 'swallow' jugs from Akrotiri, from Phylakopi and from shaft-grave Gamma at Mycenae have been found, by clay analysis, to be of Cycladic origin and it is most likely that they were made by the same potter. A pair of golden earrings found in shaft grave III is identical with those worn by one of the 'Saffron Gatherers' in the fresco from Xesté 3 at Akrotiri. The miniature paintings from the West House at Akrotiri also depict scenes the spirit of which is Mycenaean rather than Minoan. Indeed, Marinatos declared the 'admiral of the fleet', shown in the cabin of the flagship, to be a genuine Mycenaean. The weaponry of the warriors shown in the fragment from the north wall consists of long spears, long ox-hide body shields and boar's tusk helmets. The helmets are commonly known from Mycenaean tombs on the Greek mainland. Furthermore, scenes such as that of the 'Shipwreck' are much closer to the battle scenes from the Mycenaean silver vases and are completely alien to the peaceful character and spirit of Minoan art. Other details of the Theran miniature paintings showing connections with Mycenaean art have been fully discussed in recent papers by S. Immerwahr, O. Negbi and S. Iakovides. Iakovides has pointed out that these elements are 'too many, too concentrated and chronologically too close to be the result of mere chance'. Agreeing with Marinatos and Negbi that Mycenaeans had already settled in Thera at the time of the shaft graves, Iakovides has proceeded to suggest that these Mycenaeans occupied leading positions in Theran society. One such member of the élite class would have been the 'admiral of the fleet', whom Marinatos identified as the owner of the West House.

plates X, XIV

Whether specific racial characteristics can be distinguished in the figures in the miniature paintings from the West House is a matter for discussion. The presence, however, of Mycenaean elements in Akrotirian art cannot be disputed. This strongly suggests that Thera had close connections with mainland Greece even at the height of her liaison with Crete. Crete either acquiesced or was too weak a power by this time to raise any objections. The presence of Mycenaean elements at Phylakopi in Melos too suggests that the Minoan policy in the rest of the Cyclades was the same.

The Mycenaean presence in the Cyclades, so close to Crete, even in the sixteenth century BC when the Minoan thalassocracy was at its zenith, is of great historical significance. It proves that the control of the seaways was in Cycladic hands and that the islanders probably acted as middlemen between Crete, the Greek mainland and the eastern Mediterranean. (It is quite likely that they continued in this role when Mycenae later replaced Crete in the trade with the east.) Moreover, the ships on which the Mycenaean warriors are depicted in the Theran wall-paintings could only be Cretan or Cycladic. It would be too early for the mainlanders to have developed comparable skills in shipbuilding and seafaring. Thus, whether these warriors were transported by ships hired for a mission of their own, or whether they were mercenaries of Crete or a Cycladic power, it is certain that such enterprises brought them into closer contact with the system operating in the Aegean to maintain the balance of power. And, as soon as they realized the role played by the Cycladic islands, it is not difficult to surmise what their attitude would have been. No doubt like the Minoans before them they employed the islanders to act as intermediaries in their overseas trading ventures. The first seagoing Mycenaean vessels may have been built by Cycladic experts and manned by Cycladic seamen. The Mycenaeans would thus have benefited from the extensive trading links of the islanders, and the rapid expansion of Mycenaean trade influence throughout the eastern Mediterranean may be more readily understood. Already, before the end of the fifteenth century BC, Mycenaeans had founded a colony at Ialysos (Trianda) in Rhodes, and, by the end of the Mycenaean IIIA1 period, *c.* 1400 BC, Mycenaean emporia had been established in the eastern Mediterranean.

The appearance of the Mycenaeans on the stage of Aegean affairs in the sixteenth century BC surely heralded the first challenge to Minoan supremacy. The gradual Mycenaean expansion into the Aegean meant a parallel restriction of Minoan control. Finally, the spread of Mycenaean emporia in the eastern Mediterranean marked the total disappearance of the Minoans from the stage. By the middle of the fifteenth century BC the Minoan thalassocracy no longer existed and Crete was declining ever more rapidly. This decline has often been attributed to the volcanic eruption of Thera. Regardless, however, of what the effects of this eruption were on Crete, the presence of the Mycenaean element in the Cyclades before the eruption shows that the cause of the Minoan decline must be associated with the rise of Mycenaean power. Thus the reasons for the demise of Crete were primarily political and economic, and the volcanic eruption of Thera may simply have precipitated a process already well under way.

6 The end of Late Cycladic Thera

The archaeological evidence

The civilization of Thera was at its zenith when the end came, suddenly and dramatically. It is impossible to know exactly what happened, since no written records exist from the period, but archaeology has produced sufficient evidence for an attempt to be made at reconstructing some of the scenes in the final tragedy.

The absence of human skeletons from the ruins surely means that Akrotiri had been evacuated before the houses collapsed, implying that the city's inhabitants had had warning of the impending disaster. Most probably the strong, destructive shocks of the earthquake were preceded by slight tremors which made people leave their homes and run into then open countryside, the natural reaction of a populace familiar with earth tremors and volcanic eruptions. From the archaeological evidence it is clear that these minor tremors presaged a major earthquake which was then followed by a period of calm–perhaps of several months' duration–during which the townsfolk came back. The evidence for their return is quite convincing, for some of the buildings were repaired in a makeshift fashion and reinhabited. This evidence was originally interpreted by Marinatos to mean that squatters, in search of loot from the houses of the wealthy, had taken over the abandoned city. However, as the excavation has progressed, it has become clear that the renovations were substantial enough for a major reoccupation of the city by its original inhabitants to have taken place.

On top of the levelled debris in reoccupied parts of the town a number of stone tools have been found. Resembling hammers and anvils, they bear marks which show that they were used systematically to clear and demolish damaged buildings. In particular, a class of heavy stone hammer–as much as 14 kg in weight–without shaft hole, yet with clear signs of use at both ends, may have been incorporated in some kind of primitive demolition machine. The presence of a pair of grooves around each of these 'demolition' stones and small depressions suggests that ropes were tied round them–the knots being accommodated within the depressions–and they were then suspended from a structure and used in the same way as modern steel balls to knock down walls.

plate 68

Further evidence of the systematic clearing of the ruins after the earthquake comes from Telchines Road, the only fully excavated thoroughfare of the city.

Here accumulated debris had been removed and deposited in piles along the side of the street, retained by poor dry-stone walling. The path thus cleared along the street made it possible to transport materials needed in the restoration of the houses. Two clay buckets full of fresh mortar for wall-plaster were found in the upper storey of Room 4 in the West House, clearly indicating that such restorations were under way and, furthermore, that they were suddenly interrupted. Earth tremors do not seem to have been the cause of the interruption this time. It appears instead that the volcano had started to erupt. Again the absence of victims (no human or animal skeletons have been found) suggests that the Akrotirians had prior warning. Perhaps the eruption was heralded by the release of fumes and gases, which gave the inhabitants enough time to abandon the city and take their valuables with them. This is the only possible explanation for the fact that no precious objects have yet been discovered at Akrotiri. Curiously, jars full of grain have been found placed between the doors of the *polythyron* in the upper storey of Room Delta 1. Perhaps this unorthodox method of storage on an upper floor was an attempt by the residents to rescue some food in the hope that they would return.

plate 6

The second evacuation of the city was the final one. Soon afterwards the whole site, indeed the whole island, was covered with a thin layer of pellety pumice about 3 cm thick. The surface of the pumice looks like a hard crust, which suggests that after it had settled there was rain, sufficient to 'set' the pumice and form the crust but not heavy enough for the pumice to be removed. Slight oxidation observable in this layer has been explained by the specialists as the result of exposure of the pumice to the atmosphere for a period of about a few months to two years. After this time the volcano began to eject quantities of much larger pumice–often exceeding 15 cm in diameter–which were deposited over the site in several consecutive layers, probably representing corresponding paroxysms of the volcano. The cumulative thickness of this pumice deposit throughout the site varies from about half a metre to more than a metre: on top of projecting walls the pumice layer is thin, in pockets between the houses or in the streets it is thicker. The overall effect, however, was like that of snow in that the entire area was eventually more or less levelled. In some cases pumice had fallen into the houses through open or street-level windows, as in the case of Building Delta (Room 16), the West House or Xesté 3. In other cases the pumice accumulated against the closed doors where it was so tightly packed that it retained the impressions of the wooden panels even after they had disintegrated, as in the entrance to the West House, the easternmost entrance to Building Delta and several street-level windows (e. g. Building Beta, Xesté 3).

plate 9

The final phase of the eruption is recorded archaeologically by a very thick mantle of volcanic ash, known also as tephra or pozzuolana, deposited over the entire site and often exceeding 5 m in thickness, even after so many millennia of erosion. In this final paroxysm colossal basaltic boulders were ejected together with the tephra. Marinatos, having observed such boulders in the fields, spoke of 'bombs' and suggested that they must have hit the city as well. He proved to be right, for the building Xesté 4 was found to have been badly damaged by such 'bombs', which were discovered *in situ*.

In some cases the fine tephra also fell inside the houses through open windows, sometimes in such quantities that whole rooms were filled with it, which has proved a blessing for the archaeologists since everything packed within the tephra is very well preserved. Furthermore, artefacts of organic material, in particular wood, have left their 'negatives' in the ash after their slow disintegration. We have already observed how, by pouring plaster-of-Paris into the holes, exact replicas of tables, beds, stools and chairs have been cast. Other organic materials did not disintegrate and objects such as wicker or rush baskets have been recovered from the tephra deposits, albeit in powdery condition.

plate 84

Quite how long it took for Akrotiri to be buried completely is not known and cannot be proved archaeologically. Immediately the eruption commenced all human activity stopped and all signs of life disappeared. According to the vulcanologists, however, the process will have been a short one and the sequence of events quite rapid.

The void created beneath the shell of the crater finally caused the central part of the island to collapse, thus forming the caldera, but hereagain it cannot be demonstrated archaeologically whether or not this was an immediate result of the eruption. The caldera can certainly not have pre-dated the eruption, as is shown by the existence of Late Cycladic building remains very near the cliffs of the caldera and the fact that at least one of the buildings excavated at Balos by Mamet and Gorceix was cut off because of the collapse of the caldera walls.

The geological evidence

The Bronze Age eruption of Santorini is the only prehistoric eruption associated with a civilization and, therefore, the only one which can be studied with regard to its effect on that civilization. In recent years geologists and vulcanologists have shown increased interest in the volcano, and two very successful international congresses focussing on Thera have been held (1969 and 1978). The conclusions of these specialists may be briefly summarized as follows.

As we saw in chapter 1, the material deposited on the island of Thera during the Bronze Age is known as the Upper Pumice Series, to distinguish it from the other two horizons, easily recognizable in the profile of the caldera walls and dating from the very remote past, the Middle and the Lower Pumice Series. The Upper Pumice Series, as much as 60 m thick in places, consists of a basal layer of pinkish lumpy pumice, up to 5 m thick, known as Rose Pumice. On top of this layer lies a thick deposit of pumiceous ash which also contains lumps of pumice as well as fragments of older rocks. Since there is no evidence of a horizontally directed force and deposition, the Rose Pumice layer is considered to be of 'pumice-fall' origin. The tephra overlying it is in fact in two layers. The lower layer, up to 7 m thick, comprises ash bedded because of base surges (ash clouds which swept outward from the crater at high velocity). The upper layer consists of so-called 'chaotic' ash deposits, up to 50 m thick. Examination of the Rose Pumice, base-surge tephra and chaotic tephra has shown that there is no significant change in the chemistry and mineralogy from layer to layer, which implies that there was no interruption in volcanic activity, only a change in the nature of the eruption. Moreover, the absence of any stratigraphical break between the base-surge and chaotic tephra suggests that the latter layer was the result of an ash flow and not, as previously proposed, a mud flow. The presence of older rock fragments in the ash deposit is explained by the fact that the walls of the crater gradually collapsed as the eruption progressed. Some of the enormous boulders which hit prehistoric Akrotiri were of the same provenance.

Comparing the volcanic deposits found overlying Akrotiri with those in the Thera quarries and other places around the caldera, it is immediately striking that all the deposits are thinner at Akrotiri. This must be due to the distance of the site from the volcanic cone, as well as to the faster rate of erosion here than in the central part of the island.

Taking into account both the archaeological and the geological evidence, one may summarize the eruptive sequence of the volcano as follows. A series of tremors and earthquakes was followed by a relatively short period of calm. Then the eruption started, producing first a small quantity of pellety pumice. Another short period of quiescence followed, after which events developed rapidly and the various phases of the eruption became stronger and stronger. First, the Rose Pumice was produced. The final paroxysmal eruption seems to have been tremendous, ejecting enormous masses of ash into the air. According to Professors Charles and Dorothy Vitaliano, this phase of the eruption is represented on the island by the two deposits of tephra: the 7-m-thick base-surge deposit and the 50-m-thick chaotic tephra which gradually settled as an ash flow. The height to which this latter ash was expelled in the air seems to have been considerable, judging from its distribution in the eastern Mediterranean. Traces of the ash have been found on the island of Melos (in the third city of Phylakopi) and in various Late Minoan IA sites in eastern Crete (e.g. Zakros, Pyrgos). Deposits 10–30 cm thick have recently been located on the islands of Rhodes (Trianda) and Kos. This confirms the evidence from deep-sea sediment cores of an easterly to southeasterly dispersal of tephra, which means that at the time of the eruption westerly to northwesterly winds were blowing.

fig. 22

fig. 23

The ejection of huge masses of material created an enormous chamber under the earth's crust, and eventually the roof of this magma chamber must have fractured and collapsed. The area of the caldera thus formed would have been about 83 sq. km and the originally circular island would have acquired its present crescentic form, consisting of Santorini, Therasia and Aspronisi. It is impossible fully to comprehend the sheer size of the abyss created by the chamber collapse, especially when one realizes that, in places, the sea bed in the caldera is 480 m deep and the walls of the caldera rise up a further 300 m. The sea poured into this enormous void through fractures in the ring of land, in the northwest and southwest of the island. If the chamber collapse was sudden, the flow of

fig. 1

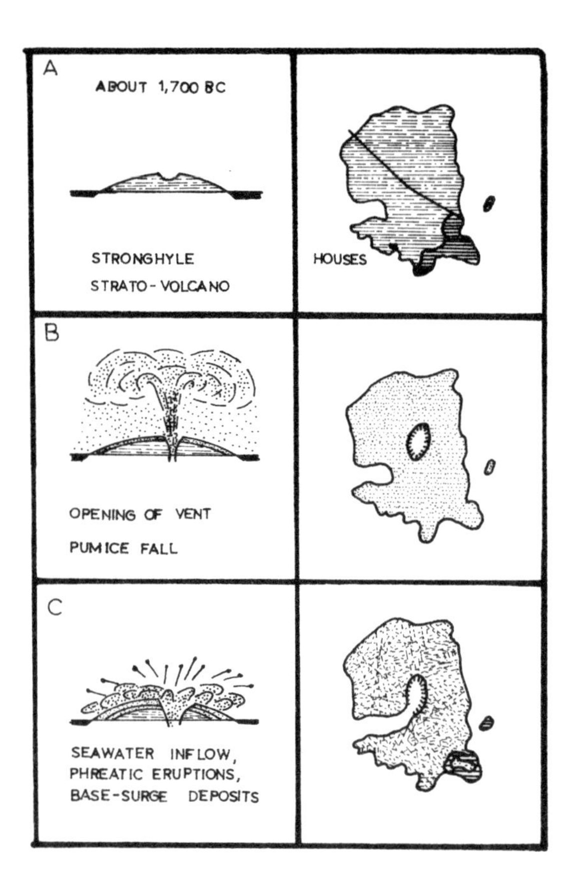

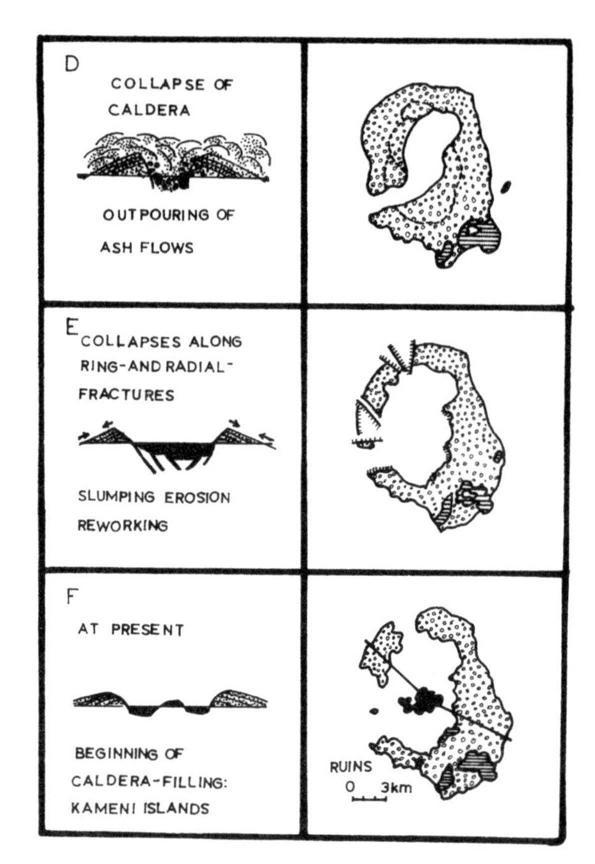

22 Diagram showing the Geological development of Thera between about 1700 BC and the present, after H. Pichler and W. L. Friedrich.
(A) The island of Stronghyle just before the Late Minoan eruption. Monolithos was still an islet east of Thera. (B) Beginning of the eruption some time before 1500 BC. The entire island of Stronghyle is covered with pumice. (C) Base surges caused by the inflow of sea water sweep away part of the pumice and deposited ashes, leaving uncovered the hilltops of Profitis Elias and Monolithos. (D) The collapse of the caldera coincides with more deposits of ash on the remaining part of the island. (E) Fragmentation of the ring creates the island of Thera, Therasia and Aspronisi. Masses of ash moved by erosion incorporate Monolithos into the island of Thera. (F) Re-activation of the volcano in later centuries gave birth to the Kameni islands in the middle of the caldera.

water must have generated tidal waves to the north and southwest. According to a more recent point of view, however, the chamber collapsed gradually, and tidal waves would therefore not have been caused.

Chronology

On the basis of stylistic examination of the pottery, the date of the disaster on Thera coincides with the completion of the development of Late Minoan IA pottery in Crete. Indeed, both imported Minoan pottery at Akrotiri, as well as local imitations, are restricted to the style prevailing in Late Minoan IA Crete; so far, pottery of the subsequent Late Minoan IB phase, the characteristic 'Marine style', is entirely absent. Having these two very distinctive and stratigraphically distinct styles as *termini post* and *ante quem,* the date of the end of Thera must be placed towards the end of the Late Minoan IA period in Crete, the absolute chronology of which is generally accepted to be *c.* 1500 BC.

The application of the radiocarbon method of dating to the site has unfortunately not been a success. The main laboratory involved, from the beginning of the excavation (1967), has been that of the University Museum, Philadelphia, Pennsylvania, USA. During the decade 1967–77 a whole series of samples were processed by this laboratory and a wide range of dates acquired. A summary of the results has been published in the first volume of the proceedings of the Second International Thera Congress (London 1978). Samples taken were divided into two classes: long-lived (charcoal or wood) and short-lived (beans, grains, shrubs), and in both cases dates have been produced for the destruction of Akrotiri with discrepancies ranging from about 1100 ± 190 BC to 2590 ± 80 BC. Some specialists think that the discrepancies may be due to gases emanating from the volcano, and more recent research has shown that this may indeed be the case, since radiocarbon dates of plants living on active volcanoes, including Thera, show similar variations.

Tree-ring dating could have provided another means of arriving at an absolute chronology, but no satisfactory wood remains have been preserved. (This is a universal problem throughout the Aegean area because of poor conditions for the preservation of timber.) More promising seems to be the chronological study of long ice cores from Greenland based on oxygen-isotope measurements, provided of course that Santorini tephra from the Late Bronze Age eruption can be identified in these ice cores.

Although scholars continue to speculate about the effects of the Thera eruption on Crete and problems of Minoan chronology, there is no doubt that the archaeological dating of this momentous event still remains the most accurate. For not only on Thera does the end of Akrotiri coincide with the end of the Late Cycladic I period, but also on Crete, the tephra vestiges are located in Late Minoan IA horizons. The remains of Santorini tephra are found in similar horizons at Phylakopi on Melos as well as at the settlement of Ialysos (Trianda) on Rhodes. All this evidence leads, once again, to the dating of the Late Bronze Age eruption of Thera at around 1500 BC.

The westerly and northwesterly directions from which the winds seem to have been blowing during the eruption suggest that the eruption occurred during the summer, when these winds prevail. This must have been just before the new harvest of crops, as the almost empty storage jars at Akrotiri indicate. The volcano could therefore have erupted in the months of June or July.

7 The Aegean and the eruption of Thera

Thera and the desolation of Minoan Crete

The discovery of the Minoans at Knossos by Sir Arthur Evans in the early years of this century brought about a profound reassessment of the pre-Homeric Aegean. K.T. Frost, of Queen's University, Belfast, tried to associate the end of Minoan civilization with the disappearance of the legendary Atlantis. However, in his two articles, 'The Lost Continent' (*The Times,* 19 February 1909) and 'The Critias and Minoan Crete' (*Journal of Hellenic Studies* 33, 1913), Frost restricted himself to the association of legend and fact, without attempting to investigate the cause of the fact, that is, the destruction of Minoan Crete.

Knossos seems to have suffered two destructions, one in the Middle Minoan IIIB period and one in Late Minoan IA, and Sir Arthur Evans originally thought that an earthquake was responsible for the latter destruction. He changed his mind, however, on reading L. Renaudin's study of the pottery found on Thera in the 1860s (published in the *Bulletin de Correspondance Hellénique* 46, 1922). Realizing that the Thera pottery belonged to the Late Minoan IA period, he began to ponder the possibility that the Thera eruption might have caused the Late Minoan I destruction of Knossos. H.R. Hall, on the other hand, insisted without much evidence that the Thera eruption and the earlier, Middle Minoan IIIB destruction of Knossos were connected.

The late Professor Spyridon Marinatos was the first actually to elaborate the theory associating the eruption of Thera with the destruction of Minoan Crete. He himself excavated several Minoan sites in Crete, all of which had been destroyed in Late Minoan I times and, being the first scholar in the field of Aegean archaeology who was aware of the possible effects of a volcanic eruption, he proposed that the Thera volcano was the cause of this widespread destruction. He put forward his theory in 1939 in a now classic article called 'The Volcanic destruction of Minoan Crete', published in the English periodical *Antiquity.* According to Marinatos, the eruption of the volcano had been accompanied by earthquakes which caused severe damage in most Minoan sites. Moreover, sites located on the north coast of Crete had been engulfed and obliterated in a very short space of time by enormous tidal waves generated by the volcano. Marinatos attempted to estimate the magnitude of the eruption from the stratigraphical evidence, the volume of material ejected and the mechanism of the formation of the Thera caldera. He sought a parallel elsewhere and the closest seemed to be a volcano in the Sunda Strait between Sumatra and Java called Krakatoa, which erupted in AD 1883. It is considered by vulcanologists to be of the same type as the Thera Late Bronze Age volcano, and an examination of the structure of both suggests that their history was not dissimilar. It is, therefore, quite logical to take into account the well-documented eruption of Krakatoa when attempting to comprehend the forces at play in the Theran eruption.

On 20 May 1883 the volcano of Krakatoa showed signs of mild activity which soon subsided, betraying nothing of what was to come. On 19 June activity started again, increasing gradually until 26 August when the first serious eruption took place at 13.00 hours. The crescendo of increasingly more severe explosions was such that within four hours, at 17.00 hours, the climax of the first collapse occurred. Activity continued throughout the night and the final paroxysmal eruption took place at 10.00 hours on 27 August, creating a cloud of ash 50 miles high. Following this collapse the explosions continued, with decreasing intensity, and by early morning on 28 August the eruption had ceased.

Two phases can be distinguished in this sequence of events. The first phase, very mild and of short duration, commenced on 28 May and can be compared with that phase of the Thera eruption which warned the inhabitants of Akrotiri to leave their homes and which ended with the ejection and fall of pellety pumice over the whole island. The second phase of the Krakatoa eruption, much more intense, lasted seventy-one days, from 19 June to 28 August, and coincides with the phase on Thera when enormous quantities of pumice and ash were ejected, covering the entire island with a voluminous mantle. Within this phase, in both instances, is included the final explosion which produced fine dust and terminated in the total collapse of the volcano.

Ships navigating the seas in the vicinity of Krakatoa reported that floating pumice in some places had formed a layer about 3 m thick. Other ships, 160 miles off, reported that they were covered with dust three days after the end of the eruption. In fact the dust cloud completely shrouded the area, so that it was dark even 257 miles away from the epicentre. The period of darkness lasted twenty-four hours in places 130 miles distant and fifty-seven hours 50 miles away. The black-out in the immediate vicinity continued for three days and was so total that not even lamp-light could penetrate it. Stunningly beautiful sunsets were observed during the winter months in both America and Europe, thanks to the suspension of fine particles of dust in the atmosphere.

Krakatoa erupted noisily. It could be heard as much as 3,000 miles away on Rodrigues Island in the Indian Ocean. Vibrations shattered shop windows 80 miles off. The energy released in the main explosion has been estimated to be equivalent to an explosion of 150 megatons of TNT. A tidal wave generated by the main collapse achieved a height of 36 m more than 30 miles away from Krakatoa and destroyed 295 villages on the neighbouring coasts of Java and Sumatra. Over 36,000 people lost their lives, mainly by drowning. The tidal wave carried the gunboat Berow about 1.9 miles inland from the harbour of Teloeg Betoeng, 50 miles north of Krakatoa.

By comparing Thera with Krakatoa Marinatos concluded that the Theran eruption must have been much stronger, since its caldera is almost four times greater than that of Krakatoa. Taking into account the distance between Crete and Thera, as well as the depth of the sea in that area, he also suggested that the tidal waves were much larger and more violent. These natural forces, according to Marinatos, caused the end of Minoan civilization. For not only were the palaces and towns destroyed, but the Minoan fleet, the basis of Minoan power, was wiped out. Marinatos enlarged on his theory in subsequent articles. The assumed total destruction of the Minoan fleet afforded the Mycenaeans of the Greek mainland an opportunity to expand. They soon captured Knossos, where a Mycenaean dynasty seems to have been established. These warlike new rulers of Knossos apparently kept the existing administrative system, adapting themselves to it. The Minoan syllabic Linear A script was used by the Knossian king for palace book-keeping. Not understanding the language disguised under the Linear A script the Mycenaean rulers employed Minoan scribes to carry on with the book-keeping, but in their own (Mycenaean) language. The scribes, in their turn, simply modified some of the Linear A signs in order to accommodate the sounds that existed in the language of the new rulers. Thus, and with the invention of a few more signs, the Linear B system of writing developed. Michael Ventris, who deciphered the Linear B script, proved that under these symbols lay hidden sounds and words of the Greek language, demonstrating therefore that the palace of Knossos was occupied by Greek-speaking people. Marinatos spelt out the possible implications of these ideas in an article with the dramatic heading, 'The Volcanic Origin of Linear B', published in *Europa* (1967). The article focussed on the cultural impact that the eruption of the Thera volcano had on European civilization, since it resulted in an old European language (Greek) acquiring a script.

Marinatos' theory about the eruption of the Thera volcano aroused controversy from the moment it was first published. Even the editors of *Antiquity* printed a note at the end of the 1939 paper expressing their scepticism. The main argument against the theory was and still is the chronological discrepancy: the eruption occurred in Late Minoan IA times, whereas the evidence for a widespread destruction in Crete is in the Late Minoan IB horizon. When Marinatos published his theory there was much confusion about the two periods and many believed–including Marinatos himself–that LM IA and LM IB styles were contemporary, although Sir Arthur Evans had already distinguished them as belonging to two different periods. Extensive work after the Second World War has confirmed Evans' distinction.

It is generally accepted that there was widespread destruction of the Cretan palaces–except the palace of Knossos–and sites towards the end of the Late Minoan IB period, or about 1450 BC. Those scholars who connect Thera with this destruction, since they cannot lower the date of the end of Akrotiri, have proposed that the eruption of the volcano happened long after the destruction and abandonment of the city. With slight modifications this view is supported by Marinatos, Page, Platon, Luce and Warren. According to them, the destruction on Crete was due to earthquakes accompanying the eruption of Thera and desolation caused by the tephra fall. As evidence for the theory it has been suggested that the piles of debris cleared from the streets at Akrotiri were soil formed after the earthquake destruction, implying a time interval of several decades (Money, Warren). Analyses have, indeed, shown that humus is present in this debris, but this still leaves many points unanswered.

First, if the ruins of the town had been exposed for some decades after the earthquake then they would surely exhibit signs of erosion–none exist. Walls in fact project sharply out of the pumice, without any smoothing, and fractures in them are found full of pumice but no other kind of debris, which one might have expected to penetrate if the walls had been exposed for a long period. Secondly, if soil had been formed it would be present all over the site and not only in those places where debris had been deposited by the rescue teams just after the earthquake. Thirdly, since there is evidence that the people came back and began to clear and rebuild, these works would have been completed and the site not abandoned and, since there would have been contacts with Crete as formerly, Marine-style vases would surely have been imported. These three points alone weaken the theory that the site was exposed for a relatively long period of time. The presence of humus among the debris can be explained easily since the mud used as building material was made from pre-destruction soil. Humus is not destroyed when soil is made into mud and its accumulation on top of the piles of debris is simply a matter of practicality: when clearing rubble the stones are removed first, piled up and then the earth shovelled on top.

That the eruption of the Thera volcano preceded the destructions in Crete is also indicated by the discovery of lumps of pumice deposited in sacred places for ritual purposes. It has been suggested (Platon, Vitaliano) that floating pumice reached the shores of Crete and was deposited in shrines as votive offerings in order to placate the divine forces which caused the eruption. Such lumps have been found in the palace of Zakros and in the Minoan villa at Nirou Chani. At Amnisos, the harbour of Knossos, Marinatos also found pumice from the Late Bronze Age eruption of Thera. Indeed, this pumice led him to propose his theory. However, this pumice was not spread at random over the ruins, but, as Dorothy Vitaliano has pointed out, 'was concentrated in a walled receptacle with a small opening well off the ground'. This detail is of paramount importance, because it proves clearly that the pumice was stored in the villa at Amnisos before its destruction and that the eruption which produced the pumice must therefore have occurred earlier.

A totally different theory concerning the date of the eruption has been put forward by the American amateur archaeologist, L. Pomerance. Disregarding pottery styles and shapes, which constitute the strongest–and so far the most accurate–method of archaeological dating, he suggests that the eruption of the Thera volcano occurred in about 1200 BC, that is, about three centuries later than is generally accepted. Taking for granted that an 'area-wide cataclysm' of enormous magnitude must have been generated by the collapse of Thera, Pomerance interprets the lack of archaeological evidence for such a cataclysm as proof that the disaster did not occur at the time suggested. On the contrary, he believes, the faint evidence of contacts between the Aegean and Egypt during the period of Dynasty XVIII (1550–1307 BC) proves that such a disaster did not occur at that period. But recent research tends to minimize the effects of the Theran eruption even within the Aegean region, and makes one very sceptical about whether tidal waves were in fact created. Thus Pomerance's hypothesis does not find much support.

In an earlier paper the author has attempted to accommodate both the destruction of Thera and the desolation of Late Minoan IB Crete, suggesting that the collapse of the central part of Thera and the formation of the caldera could have happened some time after the eruption. According to this view, the destructions in Crete were due to earthquakes accompanying this collapse and perhaps minimally to tidal waves generated by it. The resistance of the roof of the magma chamber depends on a number of factors, such as its thickness, the nature of the rock of which it is composed, the extent of fracturing and the weight of the overlying ejecta. Vulcanological experts, however, are now almost unanimous in stating that the collapse of the walls of the crater and the formation of the caldera were gradual. This is confirmed in the Akrotiri excavation where, as has already been pointed out, enormous boulders ejected from the volcano were found in situ with the tephra.

The acceptance of the concept of gradual caldera formation rules out the earlier view that the collapse of the magma chamber roof was sudden and seriously weakens the idea that Crete's destruction was due to tidal waves *(tsunamis)* generated by the sudden collapse of Thera. The Japanese word *tsunami,* the vulcanologist I. Yokoyama explained at the Second International Thera Congress (1978), actually means 'harbour wave' and describes the rise in water-level inshore. It is not, therefore, a violent wave, and may not even be noticed by ships far from the coast. Its harmful effects are restricted to coastal areas, which are flooded as the water-level gradually rises and suffer considerable damage as it retreats. However, the impact of a *tsunami* depends also on whether or not there are obstacles–rocks or islands–intervening between the source and the coast affected.

The *tsunami* destruction theory finds very little support from the archaeological evidence in Crete. Except for Amnisos, where the dislocation of ashlar blocks suggests a sea-flood, destruction in almost all the other coastal sites of Crete is, as we shall see, due to conflagration–and both together is an unlikely combination. Even though the *tsunamis* may have been as high as 200 m (Marinos, Galanopoulos) (although Yokoyama thought they were only 63 m, and Pichler and Schiering recently gave an estimate of a mere 8–10 m), it seems improbable that they would have caused damage to life and property along the whole northern coast of Crete. Also open to dispute is the proposition that the tidal waves annihilated the Minoan fleet, for this could only have happened if all the Minoan ships had been in the north-coast harbours at the time, which is highly unlikely. If we accept that Crete possessed a commercial fleet, then the ships would surely have been dispersed, either at sea or at anchor in various harbours in the eastern Mediterranean. At the time of the eruption only a few would have been in north-Cretan or Cycladic harbours and thus possibly affected by the *tsunamis*.

The supporters of Marinatos' theory place great emphasis on the effect of the ash-fall on Crete, a view which gained considerable support after the work of two American scientists–D. Ninkovitch and B. Heezen–who discovered Late Bronze Age tephra from Thera on the bottom of the Aegean Sea. Examining a number of deep-sea cores, they came to the conclusion that a cloud consisting of gas, vapours and dust, and originating from the Thera eruption, 'may have covered the whole of Crete and parts of the Peloponnesus and Asia Minor'. Following this statement a series of studies were made to discover what the effect of the dust would have been if it had fallen on Crete. From these studies, and the subsequent collection of further samples from the sea bed, certain points have become much clearer. We now know that the direction of the ash-fall was southeast and the western part of Crete was entirely unaffected; the eastern part of the island, moreover, was covered with a tephra layer no thicker than 10 cm (Vitaliano). More recent work on this latter point has led scholars to reduce the thickness of the fresh tephra layer to 1–5 cm (Thorarinsson, Watkins et al.), whilst others (Pichler and Schiering) consider the tephra molecules discovered in Late Minoan sites to be due to the use of pumice stones 'in workshops and in households'. The thickness of the ash layer is of vital importance for the acceptance or not of its destructive effect on Crete. But even those who admit the maximum estimate of 10 cm express doubts about its adverse effects, unless it was accompanied by poisonous gases. In this connection, Dorothy Vitaliano makes three telling points. First, it is highly improbable that roofs could collapse under the weight of a 10-cm thick layer of tephra, even without taking into account the fact that the inhabitants would have shovelled much of it away. Secondly, because of the configuration of the Cretan terrain and in particular combined with rainfall, erosion of this loose tephra layer would have been pronounced. Thirdly, 'amounts of ash–up to a foot or so–have often proved to be beneficial in the long run, acting to hold moisture'. Many scholars dispute, therefore, whether even the fall of tephra over eastern Crete played a part in the destruction of the Minoan sites there.

fig. 23

Since there is such a mounting body of opinion casting doubt on the role played by *tsunamis* and ash-falls in the Minoan demise, perhaps one should take a closer look at the archaeological evidence. As has already been pointed out by the major supporter of Marinatos' theory, the late Sir Denys Page, most of the sites which produced evidence of destruction in Late Minoan I times have proved that this destruction happened in the second half of the period, i.e. Late Minoan IB. From the fifteen sites listed below it also becomes clear that most of them were destroyed by fire:

Site	*Cause of Destruction*	*Period of destruction*
Amnisos	Fire and wave action	Late Minoan I
Gournia	Fire	Late Minoan IB
Hagia Triada	Fire	Late Minoan IB
Katsambas	Undefined	Late Minoan IA
Knossos	Earthquake	Late Minoan IA
Mallia	Partly fire	Late Minoan IB
Mochlos	Undefined	Late Minoan IB
Nirou Chani	Fire	Late Minoan IB
Palaikastro	Fire	Late Minoan IB
Phaistos	Fire	Late Minoan IB
Pseira	Undefined	Late Minoan IB
Sklavokampos	Fire	Late Minoan IB
Tylissos	Fire	Late Minoan IB
Vathypetro	Fire	Late Minoan IB
Zakros	Fire	Late Minoan IB

If one tries to associate these destructions with earthquakes and with the eruption of Thera, it immediately implies that the earthquakes were volcanic. But, as Dorothy Vitaliano has pointed out, 'volcanic earthquakes are very shallow... and usually very weak...they are felt only in the vicinity of an erupting volcano and seldom are strong enough to do damage even there.' It might therefore seem more likely that a tectonic earthquake (i.e. one not associated with the eruption of Thera) caused the destructions, which also accords with the chronological evidence. However, Mrs Vitaliano argues against tectonic earthquakes too, with quite good reason: why, she asks, was this earthquake so selective as to leave Knossos out? H. Pichler and W. Schiering suggest as an answer that the destructions in Late Minoan IB Crete were due to local earthquakes in the 'tectonically unstable region'. But hereagain, as Mrs Vitaliano remarks, since most of the sites show signs of destruction by fire, it would be an astonishing coincidence for all the earthquakes to have occurred at a time when oil-lamps and fires were lit; moreover, oil-lamps are not generally overturned when an earthquake happens.

From the foregoing discussion it becomes clear that many scholars now tend to dissociate the desolation of Crete from the eruption of Thera. Sinclair Hood in fact ascribes the destruction of Late Minoan IB sites to human agency, perhaps a war of conquest. As evidence he cites the generally accepted presence at Knossos of rulers from the Greek mainland. In view of what has been said in chapter 5 concerning the so-called Minoan thalassocracy–about the role of the Cycladic islands and the possible presence of Mycenaeans in Thera even before the eruption–Sinclair Hood's theory may be tenable. But a number of factors could have been at play. Natural causes–earthquakes–during the Late Minoan

IB period may simply have weakened Cretan resistance, leaving the island at the mercy of Cycladic pirates who looted and set fire to the wealthy Minoan cities. Perhaps this explains why only the eastern part of Crete–the nearest to the Cyclades–was affected. There was no need to destroy Knossos, since that palace had already been captured by the attackers. The inhabitants of eastern Crete seem to have fled westwards, to the more remote and therefore safer opposite end of the island. If the east-Cretan sites were ravaged in this way then the lack of evidence in support of Hood's theory of a war of conquest can be explained: there was no conquest but rather a complete abandonment. Comparable desolations due to piratical raids are not unknown in the history of the Cycladic islands.

Thera, the Aegean and the eastern Mediterranean

The equation of the Thera eruption with that of Krakatoa has led scholars to speculate about the likely impact of the prehistoric eruption not only in the Aegean region but also round the Mediterranean and even beyond it. Thus Mrs Vitaliano has suggested 'a more or less extensive black-out after each major explosion. . . spectacular electrical displays in the ash cloud over the volcano. . . very heavy rains and severe thunderstorms associated with the ash particles in the atmosphere, which could act as condensation nuclei for water vapor. . . noticeable lowering of temperature' because of the disappearance of the sun. She also suggested 'tremendous shock-waves or loud booms after the most powerful explosions, probably felt or heard far beyond the Mediterranean area, with some of the concussions strong enough to damage buildings within a considerable radius', and finally, 'extraordinary spectacular flaming sunsets the world over for many months after the eruption'. As we have seen, according to Ninkovitch and Heezen the initial cloud of gas, vapours and dust probably covered the whole of Crete and parts of the Peloponnese and Asia Minor. These two scholars have been more specific in estimating the radius of the roar of the explosion which 'should have been heard as far as Gibraltar, Scandinavia, the Arabian Sea and Central Africa'.

Scholars have made similar pronouncements about the effects of the tidal wave on the basis of their own varying estimates of its original height. The discovery of considerable pumice deposits on the island of Anaphi–about 15 miles east of Thera–at an altitude of 250 m implied a *tsunami* height of over 200 m. On this assumption Ninkovitch and Heezen wrote that 'the coast from Tunisia to Syria must have been inundated no more than three hours after the collapse of Strongyle island'. I. Yokoyama, on the other hand, estimated from Anaphi pumice at 40–50 m and pumice in Jaffa-Tel Aviv at 7 m that a *tsunami* of an original height of 63 m must have reached Anaphi in 10 minutes, Crete in 25 minutes (11 m high) and Tel Aviv in 105 minutes. Claude Schaeffer, the excavator of ancient Ugarit in Syria, even ascribed the destruction of the port and part of the city in the second half of the fifteenth century BC to the action of a tidal wave. Recent scientific work by Keller and Vitaliano, however, has entirely dis-

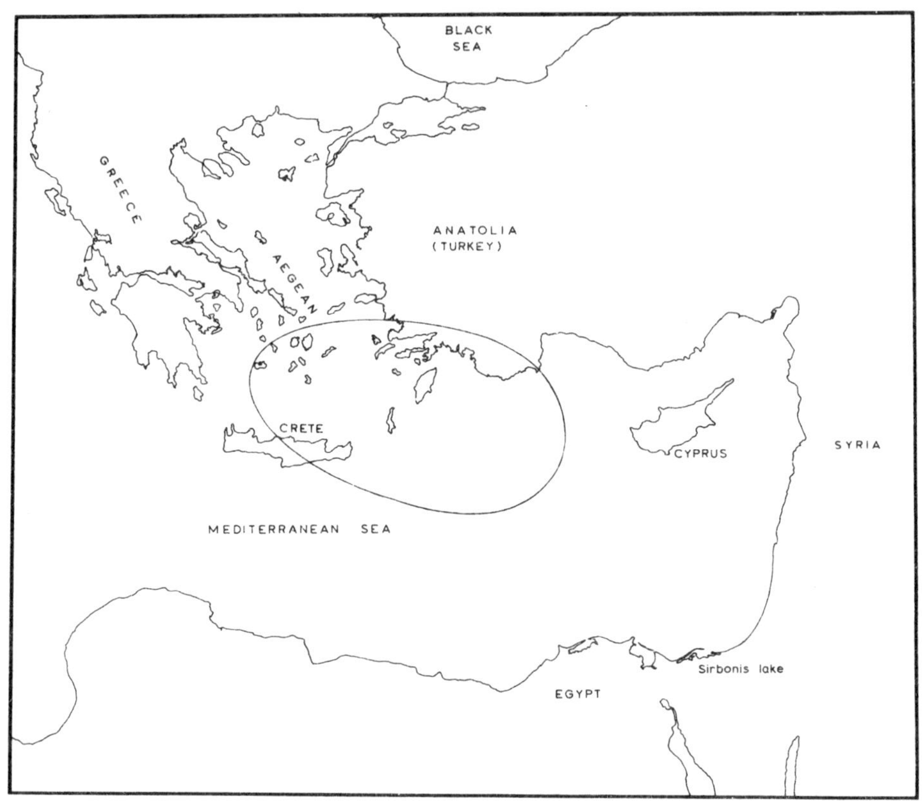

23 Distribution of ashfall from the eruption of Thera, based on evidence from deep-sea cores.

sociated the Anaphi pumice from the Late Bronze Age eruption of Thera, rendering the above estimates invalid. The recent estimate by Pichler and Schiering of the original height of the *tsunami* in any case reduces it to just 8–10 m.

fig. 23 Systematic study of the tephra deposits lying on the bottom of the sea began as early as 1947. Various scientific expeditions (Albatross 1947–48; Vema 1956, 1958; Watkins et al. 1978) have been mounted since, giving a good scatter of deep-sea cores and the following results. Tephra from the eruption was dispersed in an easterly and southeasterly direction, the axis of this dispersal passing through the island of Karpathos. The specialists (Watkins et al.) estimate a layer of 1–5 cm of fresh tephra over eastern Crete, but they point out that 'the Minoan colonies on Rhodes and the south coast of Turkey may have suffered severe tephra-fall'. This assumption appears partially to be proved by two more recent discoveries. In a survey on the island of Kos Professor J. Keller has located Santorini tephra deposits about 500 m north of Cape Phokas. The average thickness of these deposits is some 30 cm, reaching 60 cm at one point. The second discovery is at the site of Trianda (Ialysos), Rhodes. Here a recent excavation of a Late Bronze Age settlement has uncovered a layer of fine tephra about 10 cm thick. Chemical, mineralogical and refractive analysis (Keller and Vitaliano) has shown that the tephra came from the Theran eruption. But the fact that the tephra, which overlies the Late Minoan IA horizon, is immediately succeeded by subsequent horizons without any apparent break, suggests that the effect of the ash-fall on Rhodes was not very serious.

Following Marinatos' attempt to link the Theran eruption with the end of Minoan civilization, several scholars began to reinterpret the ancient myths and legends. As early as 1960 Professor Galanopoulos of the Athens Institute of Seismology associated the volcanic eruption of Thera with the legendary flood of Deukalion and the myth of Atlantis. He suggested that both legends had their origin in the tidal waves and storms which followed the great eruption. More recently the Greek scholar, N. Platon, former Professor of Archaeology at the University of Thessaloniki, presented a summary of scholarly attempts to interpret biblical and prophetic Egyptian texts as echoes of the eruption of Thera. After the end of Dynasty XVIII in Egypt texts appeared recalling, according to various experts, earlier events:

...For nine days there was no exit from the palace and no one could see the face of his fellow...

...It is inconceivable what happened in the land–to its whole extent confusion and terrible noise of tumult; oh that the earth would cease from noise...the towns are destroyed...Upper Egypt suffered devastation...blood everywhere...pestilence throughout the country....

...Men no longer sail to Byblos. What shall we do for cedar for our mummies...and for the oils with which chiefs are embalmed as far as the country of the Kefti? They come no more....

...The sun is covered and does not shine to the sight of men. Life is no longer possible when the sun is concealed behind the clouds. Ra has turned his face from mankind. If only it would shine even for one hour! No one knows when it is midday. One's shadow is not descernible. The sun in the heavens resembles the moon....

Texts with similar content are included in some of the prophets of the Bible like Zephaniah (1:15, 2:5) and Jeremiah (47:2, 4). The American historian J. G. Benett Jr and Professor Galanopoulos have recently dealt with these prophetic texts and have both concluded that they describe the consequences of the Theran eruption in Egypt and the eastern Mediterranean. Moreover, Benett has expressed the opinion that the plagues of Egypt as described in Exodus might be due to the effects of the eruption. Galanopoulos has gone one step further and connected the opening of the Red Sea and its crossing by the Jews with tidal waves generated from Thera. There are some difficulties in linking the events described in Exodus with the Thera eruption. To begin with, one has to follow those scholars who place the Exodus during the reign of Tuthmosis III (1490–1436 BC). The weak point in this dating is that Tuthmosis III several times led his armies victoriously to Palestine and Syria, thus rendering it less than likely that the Israelites would have been able to organize and attempt their Exodus. Another difficulty can perhaps be more easily overcome. Tidal waves from the Mediterranean could never have affected the Red Sea, but many scholars have suggested that the Hebrew words *Jam Suf* should be translated 'Sea of Reeds' instead of 'Red Sea'. Professor Galanopoulos identifies this 'Reed Sea' with Sirbonis Lake, a lagoon to the east of the right branch of the Nile. The route of the Exodus, as described in the Bible, favours such an interpretation, which also sounds more logical. In the biblical text (Exodus 14:21) the withdrawal of the sea was the result of a 'violent southerly wind blowing all night'. If this wind blew over the Red Sea, its withdrawal to the north is totally illogical. The two strips of land that embrace Lake Sirbonis on the north are suggested to have been the Exodus route and the mouth between them the point at which the sea was crossed.

fig. 23

Apart from the biblical and prophetic texts, scholars have also attempted to detect memories of the Theran eruption in various ancient traditions around the Aegean. These traditions, reported in a number of early sources, are local and refer to floods caused by inundations from the sea. According to such traditions, analyzed by Professor J. V. Luce, places like Attica, the Argolid, Troezen and the Saronic Gulf, Lycia, the Troad, Rhodes and Samothrace were flooded from the sea. Luce argues that the location of these places would justify an interpretation of the floods as the result of the cataclysmic tidal wave which, it has been suggested, originated from Thera.

8 Thera and the legend of Atlantis

Plato's story

Although it is difficult to estimate accurately the number of books written about the lost continent of Atlantis, E. S. Ramage, one of the most recent researchers into the subject, suggests that 'a reasonable round number seems to be 2000, though estimates range as high as 10,000'. Ramage refers, however, only to books; for, as he goes on, 'it is completely impossible to estimate the number of articles that have been written on the subject'.

None of these myriad writings would ever have been penned, nor would countless generations of archaeologists, historians, philologues and natural scientists have become obsessed with Atlantis, had it not been for one man who in about 350 BC set down the original story. This man was the great Athenian philosopher, Plato, friend and disciple of Socrates. Plato's teachings on the organization of an ideal city state governed by universal laws fill several volumes. He expounded his views in a number of works which took the form of dialogues between eminent Athenians of his day, and two of these dialogues, *Timaeus* and *Critias,* contain passages referring to the lost continent of Atlantis. In both dialogues it is Critias who relates the tale just as he had heard it from his grandfather, also called Critias, son of Dropides, who in turn had heard it from Solon, one of the seven sages of antiquity. Solon it was who travelled to Egypt from Athens in about 600 BC, visiting Sais, where Egyptian priests told him the story of Atlantis. In the first dialogue, *Timaeus,* a brief account of the story is given, while a more detailed version is presented in *Critias.*

The island of Atlantis, situated beyond the Pillars of Hercules in the Atlantic Ocean, was larger than Libya and Asia combined. A great and wonderful empire extended from this island to many others, as well as to parts of the continents as far as Tyrrhenia in Europe and Egypt in Libya. The island was created by Poseidon in order to protect his lover Cleito, daughter of Evenor and Leukippe. Two zones of land alternating with three zones of water encircled the hill on which Cleito lived. The god provided the central island with two springs, one of warm and one of cold water, and from its soil every kind of food was produced in abundance. Five sets of twin boys were born from the union of Poseidon and Cleito. Atlas, Poseidon's eldest son, became the first king of the island, which was named Atlantis after him.

As Poseidon's descendants, the rulers and inhabitants of Atlantis were favoured by the god; peace and prosperity reigned over the island, which was embellished with magnificent temples, palaces, canals, bridges and fountains. Its harbours were frequented by vessels from all parts of the world, supplying the island with all manner of goods.

Among the many special laws of Atlantis the most important was that its kings 'were not to take up arms against one another, and they were all to come to the rescue if anyone in any of their cities attempted to overthrow the royal house; like their ancestors, they were to deliberate in common about war and other matters, giving the supremacy to the descendants of Atlas. And the king was not to have the power of life and death over any of his kinsmen unless he had the assent of the ten.'

For many generations power, peace and prosperity were the hallmarks of Atlantis. For its inhabitants

> were obedient to the laws, and well-affectioned towards the god, whose seed they were ...But when the divine began to fade slowly, and became diluted too often and too much with the mortal admixture...they then, being unable to bear their fortune, behaved unseemly, and to him who had an eye to see grew visibly debased....Zeus, the god of gods, who rules according to law, and is able to see into such things, perceiving that an honourable race was in woeful plight, and wanting to inflict punishment on them that they might be chastened and improve, collected all the gods into their most holy habitation, which, being placed in the centre of the world, beholds all created things. And when he had called them together, he spake as follows:

At this point Critias' dialogue ends. One can understand, however, the end of the story from the passage in the *Timaeus:*

> ...But afterwards there occurred violent earthquakes and floods; and in a single day and night of misfortune all your warlike men in a body sank into the earth, and the island of Atlantis in like manner disappeared in the depths of the sea. For which reason the sea in those parts is impassable and impenetrable, because there is a shoal of mud in the way; and this was caused by the subsidence of the island.

How much historical truth, if any, can we perceive behind the legend? To ascertain the answer, we need to consider the geographical location of Atlantis, its extent, its degree of civilization and date of destruction, on all of which Plato is most explicit. Atlantis was an island-continent in the midst of the true ocean, beyond the Pillars of Hercules (Gibraltar). It was larger than Asia and Libya put together. Its inhabitants had developed an advanced civilization and Atlantis was the strongest naval power of all time, sovereign not only of its own island but also of others. Atlantis' authority within the Pillars of Hercules extended as far as Egypt in Libya and Etruria in Europe. This mighty and marvellous empire perished in a single day and night, some 9,000 years before Solon (who lived about 600 BC).

Agreements and disagreements

Whether Plato's account of Atlantis is fact or fiction has been a controversial issue since antiquity, dividing scholars into two opposing camps. In a recent book, edited by E. S. Ramage and with the very title, *Atlantis: Fact or Fiction?* (1979), the various arguments are summarized clearly and succinctly.

Those who maintain that Plato's story is a factual one have had to modify, correct, or even alter some of the points in the story, in particular those concerning the geographical location of the lost continent. At various times, various Atlantologists have proposed various possible sites for Atlantis, too numerous to mention. In fact, one can say without hesitation that there is practically nowhere in the world that has not been thought of as a possible home for Atlantis. As Ramage remarks, by the end of the nineteenth century the people of Atlantis had been connected 'with people as widely different in race and in time as the Goths, the Gauls, the Druids, the Egyptians and the Scyths and had been discovered in many parts of the world: the Mediterranean, the Sahara, the Caucasus, in South Africa, Ceylon, Brazil, Greenland, the British Isles, the Netherlands and Prussia.' As far as Thera is concerned, the first attempt to identify it with Atlantis was made as early as 1885 by A. Nicaise.

The great discoveries of Sir Arthur Evans at Knossos, at the beginning of the twentieth century, lent support to those who believed in the truth of Plato's narrative. K. T. Frost, as we have seen, proposed in 1909 that the Knossos civilization was none other than the civilization of lost Atlantis as described by Plato. There are indeed certain similarities which would favour this identification. Parts of the geographical description of Atlantis fit Crete, and Frost thought that the political status of Knossos was reflected in Plato's narrative. Frost continued: 'the great harbour [of Atlantis] with its shipping and its merchants coming from all parts, the elaborate bathrooms, the stadium and the solemn sacrifice of a bull are all thoroughly, though not exclusively, Minoan; but when we read how the bull is hunted "in the temple of Poseidon without weapons but with staves and nooses" we have an unmistakable description of the bull-ring at Knossos, the very thing which struck foreigners most and gave rise to the legend of the Minotaur.' However, Frost did not go so far as to connect the end of Minoan Crete with the volcanic activity of Thera, although Thera had already been linked with the story of Atlantis. This was a weak point in Frost's theory, because he failed to relate the supposed end of Atlantis 'in a single day and night' to the archaeological evidence of the demise of Minoan Crete. Instead he sidestepped the issue, writing: 'As a political and commercial force, Knossos and its allied cities were swept away just when they seemed strongest and safest. It was as if the whole kingdom had sunk in the sea, as if the tale of Atlantis were true.'

We are already familiar with the theory put forward by Marinatos thirty years after Frost, in 1939, attributing the Minoan decline to the volcanic eruption of Thera about 1500 BC. This at once removed the weak link in Frost's argument, because Crete's collapse could supposedly be shown to have been sudden. Marinatos himself later admitted a core of truth in Plato's legend. According to him, the Egyptian priests who spoke to Solon about the end of Atlantis were referring indirectly to the Late Bronze Age eruption of Thera: the complete destruction of the Minoan fleet by tidal waves resulted in a sudden break in Minoan-Egyptian contacts. Word of some of the effects of the eruption–complete darkness, ash-fall, poisonous gases, *tsunamis*–must have reached Egypt. Moreover, the rumour that an island had sunk into the sea would certainly have reached Egypt very quickly. Thus, according to Marinatos, it was not difficult for the Egyptians to confuse Thera with Crete, imagining that the submerged island was none other than the large island civilization (Crete) with which they had suddenly lost contact.

Marinatos' theory was an improvement on Frost, and it inspired Professor A. Galanopoulos of the Athens Institute of Seismology to try on geological grounds to identify Atlantis not only with Crete, but also with Thera itself. According to Galanopoulos, the two regions that constituted Atlantis–the ancient metropolis and the royal city–correspond to Thera and Crete respectively. The present circular arrangement of the islands of Thera, Therasia and Aspronisi are, according to Galanopoulos, the vestiges of one of the rings of land alternating with the circular canals surrounding the acropolis of Atlantis. The present caldera consists partly of the old canal, and the acropolis would have been on the central cone which collapsed after the Late Bronze Age eruption. The location of the ancient metropolis having thus been fixed, Galanopoulos went on to identify the royal city with central Crete. In this case the plain which surrounded the royal city was none other than the plain of Messara.

The list of modern scholars who equate Atlantis with Minoan Crete does not end with Galanopoulos. More recently, J. V. Luce, Professor of Classics at Trinity College, Dublin, and Professor N. Platon, excavator of the Palace of Zakros on Crete, have added more weight to the Cretan hypothesis of Atlantis. Luce has devoted a whole volume (*The End of Atlantis* (1969)) to the study of the Atlantis case and has concluded that there is a core of truth in the legend. Atlantis for him is the power of Minoan Crete and its disappearance means 'the end of Minoan dominance in the Aegean world'. He considers lost Atlantis as 'a historical rather than a geographical concept'. And, as far as the Late Bronze Age eruption of Thera is concerned, he states that 'what it did to Thera is comparatively unimportant in comparison with what it did to the Minoanized archipelago surrounding it, and to the Minoan heartland to the south. A brilliant and refined culture foundered under the brutal impact of Theran vulcanism. The tidal waves were the real "bull from the sea" which was sent to plague the rulers of Knossos.' The identification of Minaon Crete with Atlantis is also attempted by Professor Platon, who devoted a complete chapter of his book *Zakros* (1971) to the subject.

In his more recent contribution to the aforementioned volume, *Atlantis: Fact or Fiction?,* Luce has suggested that 'one should mentally substitute Plato for

Solon as the authority for the Egyptian provenance of the legend...'; that is, Plato himself acquired the information about Atlantis in Egypt. Luce also tries to connect the names Atlantis and Crete etymologically. It is generally accepted that 'Keftiu' was the original name for Crete. According to Luce, 'Keftiu is probably derived from a root meaning "pillar", and a western island containing a "sky-pillar", that is a lofty mountain helping to support the dome of the sky, would fit neatly into the frame of Bronze Age Egyptian mythology.' Then perhaps, Luce goes on, 'the Greek associated Keftiu with his own mythology of Atlas', thus translating Keftiu as 'Island of Atlas', Atlantis. However, Luce himself admits that there may also be some truth in the view proposed by Vidal-Naquet that the two confronted powers in the legend, Athens and Atlantis, represent in the mind of Plato the 'good' and 'bad' fates of Athens respectively. 'Good' Athens in the eyes of conservative Plato would be the city without navy, and with a well-stratified society of farmers and landowners. On the other hand, 'bad' Athens (Atlantis) 'would be a maritime state of shifty sailors and covetous merchants'.

The supporters of the Minoan Atlantis theory had to 'correct' the discrepancies between Plato's account and the actual evidence. Concerning the enormous dimensions of Atlantis as well as the high dating of its submergence (9,000 years before Solon), it has been suggested that a mistake was made by confusing the Egyptian symbol for 100 with that for 1000. Nine hundred years before Solon would be a much more acceptable date for the end of Atlantis, in fact more or less the exact date of the eruption of Thera (1500 BC). Galanopoulos, among others, also tries to explain the geographical location of Atlantis beyond the Pillars of Hercules. He suggests that Solon must have pointed out to the Egyptian priests the impossibility of accommodating such an enormous island within the Mediterranean and proposed to them that it lay in the Atlantic Ocean instead. On the other hand, Platon explains Atlantis' location in terms of the tendency on the part of the classical Greeks–after their colonial expansion in the Mediterranean–to place semi-mythical places and events beyond the Pillars of Hercules, in the Atlantic Ocean.

These corrections to, and interpretations of, Plato's account constitute part of the argument against accepting the truth of the whole story. In addition, other grounds for doubt have recently been put forward by followers of the anti-Atlantis view in *Atlantis: Fact or Fiction?* Thus, S.C. Fredericks points out that 'the alleged connection between Thera and Plato's two dialogues is both artifical and unnecessary', for Plato neither connects Atlantis with Crete nor does he mention any volcano; moreover, he speaks about the total submergence of Atlantis. Another serious argument is that 'no extant ancient Egyptian source refers to an insular maritime empire which can be identified with Atlantis or Minoan Crete', as J. Rufus Fears has remarked. The same scholar has also pointed out that the myth of Atlantis is ignored even by the Greek sources, and in particular by Plato's illustrious contemporary and friend, the orator Isocrates, in his *Panathenaic* as well as by all the authors of panegyrics of Athens.

Finally, Dorothy Vitaliano has questioned whether Cretan civilization was after all destroyed by a natural catastrophe, her detailed arguments rendering it less than likely that Crete was a prototype for the myth of Atlantis.

All the anti-Atlantis scholars agree that Plato's account is 'a poetic fancy' (Rufus Fears), or 'just another of the myths of Plato' (Vitaliano) intended to illustrate 'his theory of human history as a cyclical pattern of the rise and fall of civilizations' (Fredericks). This is further emphasized by the conclusion of the story itself, the decision of the gods to punish the sinful and arrogant inhabitants of Atlantis.

That Atlantis was a creation of Plato's imagination has already been pointed out by his greatest pupil, Aristotle, who remarked: 'The man who dreamed it up made it vanish.' Perhaps E.S. Ramage is right when he states: 'It is one of the ironies of the search for Atlantis that Plato, who lies at the centre of our intellectual tradition, now finds himself in many cases the victim of an anti-intellectual approach.'

Epilogue:
Thera and the Aegean after the eruption

Regardless of the effect of the Theran eruption on Aegean civilization, it was a momentous event and a landmark in Aegean prehistory. After 1500 BC the decline of Minoan Crete becomes more apparent and the rise of the Mycenaeans more evident. On Thera itself life apparently ceased after the burial of the island under the heavy blanket of volcanic ash. From our existing knowledge we can say that at least two centuries elapsed before the island was inhabited again. The site of Monolithos on the east coast of Thera, near the modern airport, has produced evidence of this re-occupation. Mycenaean IIIB (Late Helladic IIIB) sherds from the surface of the site demonstrate that mainlanders by that time (end of the fourteenth century BC) had re-established contacts with Thera.

As Professor Iakovides has pointed out, the fifteenth and fourteenth centuries BC are considered to be 'an era of peace and prosperity, during which Mycenaean culture had come to dominate the Aegean in every sense of the word and to exercise its influence over an area far greater than the confines of the Greek homeland.' During this long period (Late Helladic II and Late Helladic IIIA) the great Mycenaean centres, among them Mycenae, Tiryns, Thebes and Pylos, flourished on the Greek mainland. The most recent study of relations between the Aegean and the eastern Mediterranean, conducted by R.S. Merillees, has shown that it was during the reigns of Queen Hatshepsut and King Tuthmosis III that contacts with Egypt were intensified, as the Mycenaean II (Late Helladic II) pottery found in Egypt suggests. The Mycenaean colony at Ialysos (Trianda), Rhodes, was probably founded towards the end of the fifteenth century BC, that is, at the end of the Mycenaean IIB period (1450–1425 BC) or at the beginning of the Mycenaean IIIA1 period (1425–1400 BC).

The period between Mycenaean IIIB (1300–1230 BC) and IIIC1 (1230–1200 BC) is considered to be a transitional one. Many settlements on the Greek mainland were deserted and palaces at Thebes, Pylos, Gla and elsewhere were abandoned. What caused these changes in the Mycenaean world remains a mystery. One explanation links the destruction of Mycenaean sites with piratical raids by the enigmatic 'Sea Peoples', who subsequently joined forces with many dispossessed Mycenaeans to attack lands to the south and east, reaching as far as Egypt. A shift of population appears to have taken place towards Cyprus and the coast of Asia Minor. Many Cycladic islands became important centres of production for Mycenaean IIIB and IIIC pottery, with the characteristic octopus decoration. Such an important centre is now being revealed by the archaeologist's spade at Koukounaries on Paros, while another is already known at Grotta on Naxos.

The apparent prosperity of the Cyclades during the Mycenaean III period led scholars such as Sir Denys Page to associate these islands with the state of Ahhijawa mentioned in documents of the Hittites, the dominant power in Anatolia. According to Page, the importance of Ahhijawa, the capital of which he placed in the island of Rhodes, is confirmed by the fact that it was the only power that the Hittites took at all seriously.

Nevertheless, by the end of the thirteenth century BC there had been a complete change in the eastern Mediterranean, thanks to the activities of the 'Sea Peoples'. New people had already settled there; Mycenaean trade had been cut off from the east and turned increasingly to the west, where prosperous settlements continued in the northwestern Peloponnese, the Ionian islands and Italy. The breakdown in trade with the eastern Mediterranean and the shift to the west reduced the importance of the Aegean islands and marked the end of their prosperity. Several centuries were to elapse before, in the Archaic period, these islands became once again the stepping stones in a further and greater Greek expansion to the east.

Chronological table

YEARS BC	EGYPT (DYNASTIES)	CRETE	GREEK MAINLAND	NORTH-EAST AEGEAN	CYCLADES	THERA
	XIX	LATE MINOAN III 2/1	LATE HELLADIC III B/A	TROY VII	LATE CYCLADIC III B/A	LATE CYCLADIC III B
1300						
1400	AMARNA	II?	II		II	GAP
1500	XVIII	I B/A	I	TROY	I B/A	Eruption; LC IA
1600	Hyksos					
1700	XIII–XIV	MIDDLE MINOAN III B/A	MIDDLE HELLADIC	VI	MIDDLE CYCLADIC	MIDDLE CYCLADIC
1800		II B/A				
1900	XII	I B/A				
2000			EARLY HELLADIC III	TROY V		
2100	XI	EARLY MINOAN III		TROY IV	EARLY CYCLADIC III	EARLY CYCLADIC III
2200	First Interm. Period					
2300		II		TROY III		
2400	VI					
2500	V	I	I/II	TROY II	II	EARLY CYCLADIC II
2600				TROY I		
2700	IV	NEOLITHIC		POLIOCHNI		?
2800	III		NEOLITHIC	III/IV		
2900	II					
3000	I				I	
3100	PREDYNASTIC			POLIOCHNI II/III THERMI I/II		
3200						
3300				POLIOCHNI I EMPORIO IX/X		

Select bibliography

ACTA of the First International Scientific Congress on the Volcano of Thera, 1971, Athens.

COLLIER, J. 1972 *The Heretic Pharaoh,* New York.

DOUMAS, C. (ed.) 1978 and 1980 *Thera and the Aegean World,* Papers presented at the Second International Scientific Congress, Santorini, Greece, Aug. 1978, vols I and II, London.

DOUMAS, C. 1979 *Santorini,* Athens.

FRIEDRICH, W.L., PICHLER, H., KUSSMAUL, L. 1977 Quaternary Pyroclastics from Santorini, Greece and their Significance for the Mediterranean Palaeoclimate, *Bulletin of the Geological Society of Denmark* 26, 27–39.

FURUMARK, A. 1950 The Settlement at Ialysos and Aegean History c. 1550–1400 B.C. *Opuscula Archaeologica* VI, 150–271.

HOOD, S. 1978 *The Arts in Prehistoric Greece,* Harmondsworth (New York 1979).

GALANOPOULOS, A.G. and BACON, E. 1969 *Atlantis,* London and New York.

IAKOVIDES, S. 1979 Thera and Mycenaean Greece, *American Journal of Archaeology,* 83, 101–2.

IMMERWAHR, S. 1977 Mycenaeans in Thera: Greece and the Eastern Mediterranean in ancient History and Prehistory, in K.H. Kinzl (ed.) *Studies presented to Fritz Schachermeyr on the occasion of his eightieth Birthday,* Berlin, 173–91.

LUCE, J.V. 1969 *The End of Atlantis,* London and New York.

MARINATOS, S. 1939 The Volcanic Destruction of Minoan Crete, *Antiquity* XIII, 425–39

1967 The volcanic Origin of Linear B, *Europa* (Grumach Festschrift) Berlin, 204–10.

1967–73 *Excavations at Thera,* vols I–VII, Athens.

1971 *Life and Art in Prehistoric Thera,* London.

1973 *Kreta, Thera und das Mykenische Hellas,* Munich.

NINKOVICH, D. and HEEZEN, B. 1965 Santorini Tephra, in *Submarine Geology and Geophysics,* Colston Papers, vol. 17, Bristol.

PAGE, Sir D. 1963 *History and the Homeric Iliad,* London.

1970 *The Santorini volcano and the Destruction of Minoan Crete,* Soc. Prom. Hell. Stud. Supp. Paper 12, London.

PLATON, N. 1971 *Zakros, the Discovery of a Lost Palace of Ancient Crete,* New York.

PICHLER, H. and SCHIERING, W. 1977 The Thera eruption and Late Minoan IB Destructions on Crete, *Nature* 267, 819–22.

POMERANCE, L. 1970 The Final Collapse of Thera (Santorini), *Studies in Mediterranean Archaeology* vol. 26.

RAMAGE, E.S. (ed.) 1978 *Atlantis: Fact or Fiction?* Bloomington (Indiana).

VERMEULE, E. 1975 *The Art of the Shaft Graves of Mycenae,* Lectures in Memory of Louise Taft Semple, Cincinnati.

VITALIANO, D.B. 1973 *Legends of the Earth,* Bloomington and London.

WARREN, P. 1969 *Minoan Stone Vases,* Cambridge.

1979 The stone vessels from the Bronze Age Settlement at Akrotiri, Thera, *Archaeologiké Ephemeris* 82–113.

WATKINS, N.D., *et al.* 1978 Volume and extent of the Minoan tephra from the Santorini Volcano, *Nature* 271, 122–26.

List of illustrations

The majority of the photographs of the finds were taken by C. Constantopoulos, to whom the author is most grateful. Warm thanks are also extended to P. Nomikos for supplying plate 3, the German Archaeological Institute at Athens for plate 4, and to Hannibal Publications for photographs of the present excavations and of the wall-paintings.

Colour plates

AFTER PAGE 32

I View east towards the site of ancient Akrotiri.

II Triangle Square from the south.

III The 'Spring Fresco' in Room Delta 2.

IV The 'Boxing Children' fresco in Room Beta 1.

V Newly restored fresco from Xesté 3 being cleaned.

VI The 'Two Ladies' fresco from the House of the Ladies.

VII The 'Papyruses' fresco from Room 1 in the House of the Ladies.

VIII The 'Antelopes' fresco from Room Beta 1.

IX Part of the 'Blue Monkeys' fresco from Room Beta 6.

X The 'Flotilla' fresco from Room 5 in the West House.

XI Fresco showing 'banners', 'cabins' or 'palanquins' from Room 4 in the West House.

XII The 'Fisherman' fresco from Room 5 in the West House.

XIII The 'Young Priestess' fresco from Room 4 in the West House.

XIV The 'Sea Battle' fresco from Room 5 in the West House.

XV The 'River Landscape' fresco from Room 5 in the West House.

Monochrome plates

AFTER PAGE 56

1 Nea Kameni from the modern town of Phira. Photo G. Goakimedes.

2 Phira viewed from the caldera.

3 Airview of southern Thera, showing the Akrotiri region.

4 Zahn's excavations near the present site in the early part of this century.

5 Removal of topmost layer at the site of Akrotiri.

6 Excavating Telchines Road.

7 Building Gamma part-excavated.

8 The drainage system under Telchines Road.

9 Section through pumice layers.

10 View from inside of site under corrugated roof.

11 Cups fallen from an upper storey of Room 6 in the West House.

12 Pumice blocking the west propylon of Building Complex Delta.

13 Triangle Square, looking south.

14 Entrance to Room Delta 15.

15 Entrance to the West House.

16 Southwest corner of the West House.

17, 18 Water closet in the West House.

19 Entrance and staircase of Xesté 3

20 Staircase in the West House.

21 Collapsed staircase in Building Delta.

22 Storage jars in basement of Room Beta 1.

23 Storage jars in the Pithoi Storeroom of Sector Alpha.

24 Storage jars in basement of Room Delta 1a.

25 Mill installation in Room Delta 15.

26 Frescoes of the 'Boxing Children' and 'Antelopes' in Room Beta 1.

27 Fresco of one of the 'Ladies' from the House of the Ladies.

28 Detail of the 'Spring Fresco' in Room Delta 2.

29 Detail of the 'River Landscape' in Room 5 of the West House.

30–32 Fragments from the 'Saffron-gatherers' fresco in Room 3 of Xesté 3, still in the process of restoration.

33 Middle Cycladic potsherd with representation of a human face, from Akrotiri.

34 Middle Cycladic ewer from the Karageorghis Quarry. Cat. no. AKR 4859. Ht 33 cm.

35 Middle Helladic cup from Delta 16, imported from the Greek mainland. Cat. no. AKR 503. Ht 11 cm.

36 Middle Cycladic clay human figurine, from Delta 6. Cat. no. AKR 545. Ht 7 cm.

37 Middle Cycladic clay figurine in the form of a bull, from fire area north-east of Building Delta. Cat. no. AKR 598. Ht. 7.4 cm.

38 Middle Helladic jar from fire area north-east of Building Delta, but imported from the Greek mainland. Cat. no. AKR 627. Ht 40.8 cm.

AFTER PAGE 88

39 Late Cycladic clay rhyton in the form of a triton shell from entrance to West House. Cat. no. AKR 1856. L 22.4 cm.
40 Late Cycladic clay rhyton in the form of a lion's head from Room 4, West House. Cat. no. AKR 1855. Ht 11.4 cm.
41 Late Cycladic clay rhyton in the form of a bull from Alpha 2. Cat. no. AKR 563. L 24.6 cm.
42 Late Cycladic ostrich egg made into a rhyton from Delta 16. Cat. no. AKR 1854. Ht 20.1 cm.
43 Late Cycladic clay oil-lamp from Delta 2. Cat. no. AKR 1186. Ht 5.3 cm.
44 Late Cycladic brazier or incense burner from Delta 2. Cat. no. AKR 936. Ht 6.5 cm.
45 Late Cycladic clay tripod cooking pot from Delta 2. Cat. no. AKR 989. Ht 17.6 cm.
46 Late Cycladic portable clay tripod 'cooker' from Delta 17. Cat. no. AKR 1376. Ht 29.6 cm.
47 Late Cycladic local bridge-spouted pithos with painted linear decoration from Beta 1. Cat. no. AKR 1437. Ht 12.8 cm.
48 Late Cycladic imported ewer with painted linear decoration from Alpha 2. Cat. no. AKR 157. Ht 22.5 cm.
49 Late Cycladic local bridge-spouted ewer with dark-on-light floral motifs from Alpha 2. Cat. no. AKR 207. Ht 18.5 cm.
50 Late Cycladic local beak-spouted ewer with dark-on-light floral motifs from Delta 2. Cat. no. AKR 1470. Ht 36.5 cm.
51 Late Cycladic local ewer with dark-on-light floral motifs from Alpha West 2. Cat. no. AKR 928. Ht 213 cm.
52 Late Cycladic local jug with dark-on-light floral motifs from Delta 2. Cat. no. AKR 1248. Ht 15 cm.
53 Late Cycladic local flower vase with light-on-dark floral motifs from Delta 8. Cat. no. AKR 1279. Ht 25.5 cm.
54 Late Cycladic local strainer with light-on-dark floral motifs from Alpha 2. Cat. no. AKR 562. Ht 23.9 cm.
55 Late Cycladic imported ewer with dark-on-light floral motifs from Delta 1. Cat. no. AKR 1253. Ht 40.8 cm.
56 Late Cycladic imported rhyton with dark-on-light floral motifs from Delta 9, 1. Cat. no. AKR 1494. Ht 29.4 cm.
57 Late Cycladic local vase *(kymbe)* decorated with dolphins from Beta 2. Cat. no. AKR 100. L 43.2 cm.
58 Late Cycladic local breasted ewer decorated with swallows from Delta 9, 1. Cat. no. AKR 1516. Ht 43.5 cm.
59 Late Cycladic local ewer decorated with dolphins from Beta 2. Cat. no. AKR 112. Ht 18.4 cm.
60 Late Cycladic plastered offering table decorated with dolphins from West House 4. Cat. no. NAM 1974. 23. Ht 30 cm.
61 Late Cycladic local vase decorated with grapes from Delta 4. Cat. no. AKR 623. Ht 50.1 cm.
62 Late Cycladic breasted ewer from Delta 2. Cat. no. AKR 1107. Ht 28.5 cm.
63 Late Cycladic breasted ewer from Delta 4. Cat. no. AKR 877. Ht 54.9 cm.
64 Late Cycladic clay 'barbecue' from Delta 2. Cat. no. AKR 1463–64. L 38.2 cm.
65 Late Cycladic marble vase from Delta 16. Cat. no. AKR 1831. D 16.2 cm.
66 Late Cycladic sealstone with a griffin from Delta 16.
67 Late Cycladic marble chalice from Delta 16. Cat. no. AKR 1829. Ht 20.3 cm.
68 Late Cycladic stone 'demolition ball' with grooves made for the ropes used to suspend it from Mill Square. Cat. no. AKR 479. L 31.6 cm.
69 Late Cycladic stone mortar from Delta 2. Cat. no. AKR 882. Ht 14.2 cm.
70 Late Cycladic stone oil-lamp from Delta 1. Cat. no. AKR 1420. Ht 12.1 cm.
71 Late Cycladic stone pestle and mortar from Gamma 1. Cat. no. AKR 484/630. Ht 11.3 cm, L 9.5 cm.
72 Late Cycladic stone 'bird's nest' bowl from Delta 16. Cat. no. AKR 1835. Ht 10 cm.
73 Lead balance weights.
74 Bronze tools and weapons.
75 Undecorated bronze ewer from Delta 3. Cat. no. NAM 1974. 5. Ht 52 cm.
76 Reconstruction drawing of decorated bronze ewer from Delta 3. Cat. no. NAM 1974.7.
77 Bronze scale pans.
78 Bronze baking pan from Delta 3. Cat. no. NAM 1974.6. Ht 7.6 cm.
79 Bronze spouted cup from Delta 3. Cat. no. NAM 1974.2. Ht 8 cm.
80 Bronze 'frying pan' from Delta 2. Cat. no. NAM BE 1974.8. Ht 14.8 cm.
81 Lentoid clay loom weights, found in groups of several dozen with debris fallen from the upper storeys.
82 Impressions of matting on fragments of Middle Cycladic pottery.
83 Remains of a wicker basket, preserved in a cocoon of volcanic ash, in Alpha Mill House. Cat. no. NAM BE 1974.24. Ht 20.8 cm.
84 Cast of a small table from Delta 1a.
85 Base of a jar with snail-shells from Alpha 2. Cat. no. NAM BE 1974.25. Ht 13.7 cm

Figures

1 Map of the Thera island group, showing main sites and place-names, p. 10.
2 Map of the Akrotiri region, together with the possible site of the ancient harbour, p. 13.

3 Map showing main sites and placenames in the Aegean region, p. 17.
4 Diagram showing the stratigraphy of ancient soils on Thera, p. 19.
5 Plan of the excavated buildings at ancient Akrotiri, 46–47.
6 Ground plan of the West House, p. 49.
7 Ground plan of Xesté 3, p. 51.
8 The bath tub found in Room 4 of the West House, p. 55.
9 Plan of Building Beta, showing the location of the frescoes, p. 79.
10 Plan of the West House and Building Complex Delta, showing the location of the frescoes, p. 80.
11 Plan of the House of the Ladies, showing the location of the frescoes, p. 81.
12 A conjectural reconstruction of Room 5 in the West House, looking east, pp. 86–87.
13 Middle and Late Cycladic pottery from Akrotiri, p. 107.
14 Late Cycladic pottery from Akrotiri, p. 109.
15 Late Cycladic pottery from Akrotiri, p. 111.
16 Decorative patterns on Akrotiri pottery, p. 113.
17 Middle Cycladic stone jar from Akrotiri, p. 115.
18 Reconstructed tripod table from Room Delta 1, p. 116.
19 Pottery bee-hive from Room Delta 17, p. 119.
20 Detail of the 'Flotilla' fresco in Room 5 of the West House, pp. 120–21.
21 Detail of the 'Flotilla' fresco (central section), pp. 122–23.
22 Diagram showing the geological development of Thera between about 1700 BC and the present, p. 138.
23 Distribution of ashfall from the eruption of Thera, based on evidence from deep-sea cores, p. 148.

Index

Bold-face numerals refer to text figures; *italic* numerals indicate plates

Aegean, Bronze Age 22–24; climate 16–18; contacts with Akrotiri 42–43; decline 157–58; effects of the Thera eruption 147, 150; geological history 15; Minoan expansion 126–27; Mycenaean expansion 133; mythology 18–21; Neolithic 22; trade 25–26, 118, 119; writing 120–21
Aegina 15, 126
African plate 15
agriculture 118, 129
Ahhijawa 158
Akrotiri 7, *3*; art 130; Bronze Age 25, 27–28; Early Cycladic 42–44; earthquake destruction 44, 143; evacuation 134–35; excavations 12–14, 29–42, *5–25, I*; furniture 116–17, **18**; harbour 55–56; Late Cycladic city 45–125; metallurgy 114–16; metric system 121–22; Middle Cycladic settlement 42–44, 45; Minoan influences 127, 128; modern town 11, *4*; pottery 108–12, **13–16**; situation 11, 12; social organization 122–25; stone-carving 114, **17**; town plan 50, 124; trade 26, 42–43, 118–20; volcanic deposits 135–37; wall-paintings 56–108; weaving 117
Alişar Hüyük 126
Amnisos 143, 144, 146
Amorgos 18, 126, 127
Anaphi 18, 147, 148
Anatolia 22, 23, 24
Anghelidis, Stavros 31
animals, husbandry 118; on pottery 123; wall-paintings 74–75, 77, *XV*
'Antelopes' 74, 75, *26, VIII*
Antiparos 22, 24
Antiquity 11, 140, 142
Apollonius of Rhodes 127
Arabia 127
Archanes 25
Archangelos 27
architecture, Akrotiri 43–44, 50–55
Argolid 25, 150
Aristotle 156
art, Cycladic 25; Mycenaean influences 132; *see also* wall-paintings
Arvanitis, Stathis 12, 55
ashlar masonry 52
Asia Minor 126, 145, 157
Aspronisi 15, 137, 154, **22**
Athens 127, 155
Atlantis 9, 140, 149, 151–56
Attica 25, 120, 127, 150
Ayia Irini 25, 130; clay tablets 121; Cretan influences 127; destruction 44; lead weights 122; Middle Helladic pottery 26, 42; silver 128
Ayia Photia 25
Ayois Kosmas 25

Badisches Landesmuseum, Karlsruhe 27
Balkans 24
Balos 45, 136
Baltoyiannis, Stavros 41
basalt boulders 135–36
basements 51, 53–54, *22–24*
basketry 117, 136, *83*
bath-tubs 54, 110, **8**
bathrooms 54–55, 56, 82, 83
bee-hives **19**
Benett, J.G. Jr, 149
Benzi, M. 88–105
Bible 149–50
Black Sea 18, 19
'Blue Monkeys' 31, 73, 74, *IX*
boar's tusk helmets 87–88, 106, 132
Boghazköy 126
'Boxing Children' 73, 74, 75, 78, *26, IV*
Brauron 25
braziers 84
bronze 115, 117, 120, *74–80*
Bronze Age 22–28, 126–33
Building Alpha 48
Building Beta 48, 53, **9**, *23*; lavatory 55; wall-paintings 73, 74, 75, 78–79, *26, IV, VIII, IX*
Building Complex Delta 48, 53, 135, *12–14, II*; basement *22*; baskets 117; lavatory 55; mats 117; mill installation 54, *25*; staircase *20*; wall-paintings 73, 75, 76, 79–81, *28, III*; windows 51
Building Gamma 48, 79, *6, 7*
building methods 51–52
buildings 124; architecture 50–55; excavation 29–31, 48–49

caldera 7, 136, 137–38, 144, **22**
Carians 129
Chios 23
Christiana 27
chronology, Thera disaster 138–39
clay, pottery 110
clay tablets 9, 121
climate 16–18
colours, wall-paintings 56
'The Coming of Spring' 7–8, 31–41, 76, 77, 80–81, *III*
Corfu 127
counting 121–22, 128
croftsmen 124–25
Crete 11, 18; *see also* Minoan civilization
Cyclades, Bronze Age 23, 24–27, 126, 127–28, 129–31; climate 16, 18; contacts with Minoan Crete 130–31; lapidary art 43; metallurgy 114; Minoan colonization 126–27, 129–30; Mycenaean presence 132, 157–58; pottery 123; prehistoric trade 22; writing 120
Cyprus 20, 126, 157

dacite 120, 125
Dardanelle Straits 13, 18
Davies, J. 128
decoration, pottery 110–12, 123, **16**, *47–63*
deep-sea cores, analysis 148, **23**
Delos 20, 126, 127
Deukalion 149
Dia 16
diet 118
Dodecanese 24
doors 52, 135
drainage systems 50, 124, *8*
Dritsas, Panayiotis 31
dyeing textiles 117

earthquakes 44, 51, 124, 134, 137, 140, 146
Egypt, after-effects of the Thera eruption 149–50; and the Atlantis legend 151, 154–55; contacts with Mycenaeans 157; contacts with Thera 120; trade with Minoans 126, 130, 144
Epidaurus Limera 127
Etesian winds 17
Eurasian plate 15
Evans, Sir Arthur 23, 121, 140, 142, 153
Exodus 149–50

Favatas 12
figurines, pottery *36, 37*
'Fisherman' 41, 75, 78, 84–85, **12**, *XII*
floors 52–53, 117
'Flotilla' 74, 75, 77, 105–6, 118, **12**, **20**, **21**, *X*
flowers, decorative motifs on pottery 112, *49–56*
fossil plants 18
Franchthi cave 22
Fredericks, S.C. 155, 156
frescoes, *see* wall-paintings *and under individual titles*
Friedrich, Dr W.L. 18, **22**
Frost, K.T. 140, 153–54
furniture 43, 116–17, 136, **18**, *84*
Furumark, Arne 27, 110, 128, 130

Gaertringen, Baron Hiller von 12
Galanopoulos, A. 144, 149, 154, 155
geology 15–16
geometric designs, pottery 111, 123; wall-paintings 74
German Archaeological Institute, Athens 12
Gilliéron brothers 8
gold, 115, 116
Gorceix 136
Gournia 146
graves, Middle Cycladic 28
Greece, contacts with Thera 28, 42, 119, 120; Cycladic colonies 24; under Mycenaeans 157; Neolithic 22; trade with Crete 44; trade with the Cyclades 25, 26
Greek Archaeological Society 13
Greek Civil War 11
Greek language 142
Grotta 25, 158
gypsum 119

Hagia Triada 146
Hall, H.R. 140
harbour, Akrotiri 55–56
Hatshepsut, Queen of Egypt 130, 157
Heezen, B. 145, 147
Hellespont 18
helmets, boar's tusk 87–88, 106, 132
Herakleion 16
Herodotus 20, 129, 130–31
Hissarlik 23
Hittites 158
Homer, *Iliad* 126
Hood, Sinclair 146–47
'horns of consecration' 54, 76, 125
House of the Anchor 51, *13*
House of the Ladies 48, 52, 53, **11**; lavatory 55; wall-paintings 30–31, 41, 73, 74, 75, 81–82, 125, *27, VI, VII*

Iakovides, S. 85, 132, 157

Ialysos (Trianda) 127, 133, 139, 148–49, 157
Iasos 126
ice cores, dating 139
Immerwahr, S. 132
International Conferences on Thera, First, 1969 8–9, 136; Second, 1978 136, 139, 144
Ionian Islands 158
Ios 18, 129
Isocrates 155
Israelites 149–50
Italy 158

Java 141

Kalliste 7, 20
Kalymnos 24
Kamaras 12
Kamares ware 26, 28, 43, 126
Kanakis, Zacharias 13
Karageorghis quarry 28, *34*
Karpathos 148
Kastri 25, 44, 126, 127
Katsambas 146
Kea 25; clay tablets 121; climate 18; destruction 44; Minoan influences 127; Neolithic 22, 24; pottery 26, 126
Keller, J. 147–49
Kephala 22, 24
Kimolos 15
King George I (volcano) 16
Kleidi 26
Knossos 13, 22, 119, 126, 140, 142, 146–47, 153, 154
Koloumbos 16
Kos 15, 126, 137, 148
Koukounaries 158
Krakatoa 141–42, 147
Krissa 126
Kythera 25, 44, 126, 127
Kythnos 18

'Ladies gathering Saffron' 73, 76–77, 78, 106–8, 125, 132, *30–32*
landscapes, wall-paintings 75, 77, *29, XV*
lapidary art, *see* stone carving
Laurion 120
Laurium 128
lava, deposits 16; stone-carvings 43
lavatories 50, 54, 56, *17, 18*
lead 120
lead weights 115, 121, *73*
'leatherware' 26, 42, 131–32
Lelegians 129
Lemnos 23, 24
Leo III the Isaurian, Emperor 16
Lerna 25, 26, 126
Leros 16
Lesbos 16, 23, 24
Libya 88, 105
'Lilies' 75, 125
Linear A script 9, 121, 142
Linear B script 142
Luce, J.V. 143, 150, 154–55
lustral basins 49, 54, 73, 76, 106, 125, *30–32*
Lycia 150

Macedonia 22, 24
Mallia 146
Mamet 12, 136
Marathon 25
Margaritoff, Tassos 31, 41
Marinatos, Spyridon 7–8, 48, 77, 120, 134; associates eruption of Thera with the destruction of Minoan Crete 7, 15, 140–2, 145, 149, 153–54; on the eruption 135–36; excavations at Akrotiri 11–13, 29–41; and the wall-paintings 77–88, 105, 106, 132
matting 117; *82*
Mavro Rhachidhi 55–56, **2**
Mavromatis quarry 45
Mediterranean, effects of the Thera eruption 147; Minoan expansion 126, 127; Mycenaeans in 132, 133
Megalochori 12
Megara 127
Melos 15, 25; ash deposits from Thera eruption 137, 139; clay tablets 9, 121; destruction 44; Minoan influences 127, 128; obsidian 22, 114, 119; pottery 26, 126, 131–32
meltemi 17
Merillees, R.S. 130, 157
Mesa Vouno 16
Mesovouna 55, **2**
Messenia 26
metallurgy 114–16
Methana 15
metric system 121–22, 128
Michaelidis, Iakovos 31
Mikra Kameni 16
Miletus 126
Mill House 52, 54, 55, 117
mill installations 54, 118, *25*
miniature frescoes 75–76, 83, 85–105, 132, *X, XIV*
Minoan civilization (Crete) 23, 53, 88, 106; artistic influences 123, 124, 129; and the Atlantis legend 153–56; Bronze Age 23; contacts with Cyclades 130–31; contacts with Thera 42, 119, 120; Cycladic colonies 24; decline 133; earthquake destruction 44; expansion in the Aegean 126–27, 129–30; metallurgy 114; metric system 121–22; mythology 18–19, 21; Neolithic 22; palaces 124; pottery 112, 119, 123, 126; religion 125; seals 114; snails 118; stone vases 114; and the Thera eruption 7, 8–9, 11, 15, 139, 140, 142–47, 149; trade 25, 26–27, 43, 44, 126; volcanic ash deposits 137; wall-paintings 56, 74; writing 120–21
Minos, King 126–27, 129, 130–31
Minyan ware 24, 26, 42–43
Mirabello, Gulf of 127
Mochlos 25, 146
Monemvasia 127
Money 143
Monolithos 157, **22**
mosaics 53
murex shells 53, 117
Mycenae 23, 88, 127; contacts with Thera 114, 120, 131–33; expansion of 142, 157–58; pottery 26; trade 130
mythology 18–21, 126–27, 149–50

National Archaeological Museum, Athens 9
Naxos 16, 20, 25, 110, 126, 158
Nea Kameni 15, 16, *1*
Nea Makri 25
Negbi, O. 132
Neolithic 22, 24, 126
Nicaise, A. 153
Ninkovitch, D. 145, 147
Nirou Chani 143, 146
Nisyros 15

obsidian 22, 43, 114, 119, 126

'offering tables' 54, 76, 116–17, 125, **18**, *60*
Oia 129

Page, Sir Denys 143, 145, 158
painting, on pottery, 112; *see also* wall-paintings
Palaea Kameni 15, 16
Palaia Kokkinia 25
Palaikastro 146
Palestine 119, 150
Paroikia 25, 26, 42
Paros 25, 26, 42, 126, 127, 158
Patmos 16
Pelekis, Elias 12
Peloponnese 18, 21, 22, 127, 145, 147, 158
Perrakis, Stamatis 31, 41
Petruso, K. 121–22
Phaistos 121, 146
Phira 27, *1, 2*
Pholegandros 15, 18
Phylakopi 21 130; ash deposits from Thera eruption 137, 139; clay tablets 9, 121; destruction 44; Minoan influences 127–28; Mycenaean influences 132; pottery 26, 42, 132
Pichler, H. 144, 145, 146, 148, **22**
pigments, wall-paintings 56
pillars 53
pithoi 43, 53–54, 110, 114, **17**, *47*
Pithoi Storeroom 51, 52, 53–54, *24*
plants, decorative motifs on pottery 112, *49–56*; fossils 18; wall-paintings 81–82
plaster 53, 56
Plato 151–56
Platon, N. 143, 149, 154, 155
Pliocene Age 15
Poliochne 23, 24, 25
Polyaigos 15
polythron 53
Pomerance, L. 143–44
Pompeii 7
Poros 15
'Porter's Lodge' 77
Potamos, Valley of, 12, 45
pottery 73; Akrotiri 108–12, 124–25, **13–16**; bee-hives **19**; Bronze Age 24; Cycladic 25, 26, 27, 42, 43–44, 45, 117, 13–15, *33, 34, 36, 37, 39–64*; decoration 110–12, 123, **16**, *47–63*; Helladic 26, 128, *35, 38*; imported 119; Kamares ware 26, 28, 43, 126; mat impressions 117, *82*; Melos 128; Minoan 126, 128, 138–39; Minyan ware 26, 42–43; Mycenaean 157; Naxian 110; potter's marks 120
pozzuolana 135–36
Profitis Elias 15, **22**
Pseira 25, 146
pumice 16, 135, 136–37, 141, 143, **4**, *9, 12*
Pylos 126
Pyrgos 137

quarries 128–29

radiocarbon dating 139
Ramage, E.S. 151, 153, 156
Red Sea 149–50
Renaudin, L. 140
Rhodes 19, 126, 150; ash deposits from Thera eruption 137, 139, 148–49; climate 16; Minoan colonization 127; Mycenaean colony 133, 157, 158
rhytons 54, 76, 110, 119–20, 125, *39–42, 56*
'River Landscape' 75, 105, **12**, *29, XV*
rock-cut chambers 42
roofs 53
Room of the Lilies 7–8, 54, 76
Room of the Papyruses 82
Rufus Fears, J. 155, 156

'Saffron-gatherers', *see* 'Ladies gathering saffron'
Sakellariou, Mrs A. 105
Saliagos 22, 24
Saliveros, Georgios 12
Samikon 26
Samos 25
Samothrace 150
Santorini 20, 137
Saronic Gulf 127, 150
Schachermeyr, Professor 124
Schaeffer, Claude 147
Schiering 144, 145, 146, 148
Schliemann, Heinrich 23, 131
'Sea Battle' 85–86, **12**, *XIV*
sea-bed, deep-sea cores, 148, **23**; tephra deposits 148–49
'Sea Peoples' 157, 158
seals, stone 114, *66*
Second World War 11
Seriphos 18
Seteia 25
sewers 50, 124
shaft-graves, Mycenae 131–32
ships 118–19, 125, 132–33; wall-paintings 74, 75, 77, 105–6, **12**, **20**, **21**, *X*
Sicily 127
Sikinos 18
silver 115, 116, 120, 128
Siphnos 25, 120, 127
Sirbonis Lake 150
Sklavokampos 146
Skyros 22
snails 118, *85*
social organization 122–25
Solon 151, 152, 154, 155
Souda, Bay of 127
'Spring Fresco', *see* 'The Coming of Spring'
squares 50, 124
staircases 52, *19–21*
stone carvings 25, 43, 114, 125, **17**, *65–72*
stone tools 114, 125, 134
Strabo the Geographer 15
streets 50, 124
Stromboli 20, 81
Stronghyle 15, 20, **22**
Stucchi, S. 88
Sumatra 141
Sumer 79
Sunda Strait 141
Syria 119, 126, 127, 150
Syros 25

tables, tripod 116–17, **18**, *84*
Tel Aviv 147
Telchines 126
Telchines Road 9, 48, 50, 134–35, *6, 8*
Telos 24
tephra 128, 129, 135–37, 139, 145, 148–49
Theia 15
Theophanes 16
Thera, after the eruption 157–58; and the Atlantis legend 153–56; Bronze Age 25, 27–28; chronology of the disaster 138–39; climate 18; cultural links with Mycenae 131–33; effects of the eruption 147–50, **23**; evacuation 134–35; Late Cycladic

128–29; links between eruption and destruction of Minoan Crete 7, 8–9, 11, 15, 139, 140, 142–47, 149; mythology 20–21; trade 26; Venetian occupation 11; volcanic eruptions 7, 15–16, 133, 135–38, **22**, *1*
Thera Archaeological Museum 12
Therasia 15, 137, 154, **22**
Therme 23, 25
Theseus 20
Thessaly 22
Thorarinsson 145
Thorikos 126
Thorpe-Scholes, Mrs K. 119
Thrace 22, 24
Thucydides 129, 131
tidal waves 138, 140, 141, 142, 144–45, 147–50, 154
timber, in buildings 51
tools, bronze 115, *74*; stone 114, 125, 134
town plan, Akrotiri 50, 124
trade 130; Akrotiri 118–20; Bronze Age 23, 25–27; Crete 126
tree-ring dating 139
Trianda (Ialysos) 127, 133, 139, 148–49, 157
Triangle Square 51, *13, II*
tripod tables 116–17, **18**, *84*
Troad 23, 24, 150
Troezen 150
Troy 18, 23, 24, 25
Turkey 16, 148
Tuthmosis III, King of Egypt 130, 149–50, 157
Tylissos 146

University Museum, Philadelphia 139

Vathypetro 146
Venetians 11, 20
Ventris, Michael 142
Vermeule, Emily 131
Vesuvius 7
Vidal-Naquet 155
Vitaliano, Dorothy 137, 143, 145, 146, 147–48, 149, 156
volcanoes, Aegean arc 15; Krakatoa 141–42; the Thera eruption and its consequences 135–38, 147–50, **22**, **23**

wall-paintings 7–8, 49, 56–108, 123, 124, *26–32, III–XV*; excavation 31–41; Mycenaean influences 132; restoration 31, 41–42, *V*
walls, plaster 53
Warren, Peter 81, 114, 119, 143
warriors, wall-paintings 85–105, 132, *XIV*
water closets 50, 54, 56, *17, 18*
Watkins, N. D. 145, 148
weapons, bronze 115, *74*; wall-paintings 132
weaving 117, *81*
West House 12, 31, 48–49, 135, **6, 10,** *11, 13, 15, 16, II*; baskets 117; bathroom 54–55, **8**; lavatory 50, *17, 18*; mats 117; roof 53; staircase *21*; wall-paintings 41, 55, 73, 74, 75–76, 77, 82–106, 132, **12, 20, 21,** *29, X–XV*
'white storms' 17–18
windows 50–51, 52, 53
winds 17–18
workshops 53–54, 124
writing 120–21, 128, 142

Xesté 2 49, 52
Xesté 3 49, 52, 53, 135, **7**; lustral basin 49, 54, 125; staircase *19*; wall-paintings 73, 74, 76–77, 106–8, 132, *30–32*
Xesté 4 49, 52, 53

Yokoyama, I. 144, 147
'Young Priestess' 73, 75, 78, 83–84, *XIII*

Zachariou, Photis 41
Zahn, R. 12, 45, *4*
Zakros 137, 143, 146
Zapheiropoulos, Nikolaos 12